PrincetonReview.com

T0120390

ESSAYS

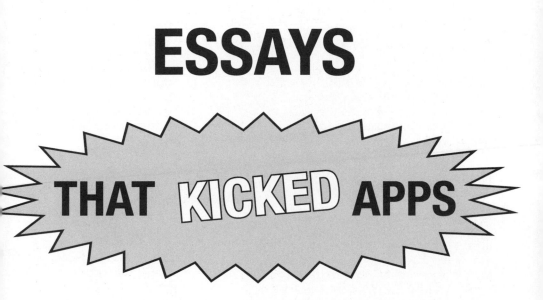

THAT KICKED APPS

Presented by the Staff of The Princeton Review

Penguin
Random
House

The Princeton Review
110 East 42nd Street, 7th Floor
New York, NY 10017

Copyright © 2023 by TPR Education IP Holdings, LLC. All rights reserved.

Published in the United States by Penguin Random House LLC, New York.

Some of the content in *College Essays That Kicked Apps* has previously appeared in *College Essays That Made a Difference* and *Complete Guide to College Essays*, both published as trade paperbacks by Random House, an imprint and division of Penguin Random House LLC, in 2014 and 2020 respectively.

All essays in this book have been reprinted with the permission of their authors.

Terms of Service: The Princeton Review Online Companion Tools ("Student Tools") for retail books are available for only the two most recent editions of that book. Student Tools may be activated only twice per eligible book purchased for two consecutive 12-month periods, for a total of 24 months of access. Activation of Student Tools more than twice per book is in direct violation of these Terms of Service and may result in discontinuation of access to Student Tools Services.

ISBN: 978-0-593-51738-3
eBook ISBN: 978-0-593-51739-0

The Princeton Review is not affiliated with Princeton University.

Editor: Aaron Riccio
Production Editor: Nina Mozes
Production Artist: Deborah Weber
Content Contributors: Julia Moody, Emily Wieweck

Printed in the United States of America.

10 9 8 7 6 5 4 3 2 1

THE PRINCETON REVIEW PUBLISHING TEAM
Rob Franek, Editor-in-Chief
David Soto, Senior Director, Data Operations
Stephen Koch, Senior Manager, Data Operations
Deborah Weber, Director of Production
Jason Ullmeyer, Production Design Manager
Jennifer Chapman, Senior Production Artist
Selena Coppock, Director of Editorial
Orion McBean, Senior Editor
Aaron Riccio, Senior Editor
Meave Shelton, Senior Editor
Chris Chimera, Editor
Patricia Murphy, Editor
Laura Rose, Editor
Isabelle Appleton, Editorial Assistant

RANDOM HOUSE PUBLISHING TEAM
Tom Russell, VP, Publisher
Alison Stoltzfus, Senior Director, Publishing
Brett Wright, Senior Editor
Emily Hoffman, Assistant Managing Editor
Ellen Reed, Production Manager
Suzanne Lee, Designer
Eugenia Lo, Publishing Assistant

For customer service, please contact **editorialsupport@review.com,** and be sure to include:

- full title of the book
- ISBN
- page number

Acknowledgments

To the wonderful students who shared their experience not just once (with colleges) but twice (with future essay writers), this book would not have been possible without you.

To the College Admissions Counseling team at The Princeton Review, with special thanks to Julia Moody and Emily Wieweck, your advice and expertise has been invaluable in helping to spotlight key strengths of these essays. We also appreciate the attentive review given to these pages by Nina Mozes and Laura Rose.

And to our outstanding Director of Production, Deborah Weber, who sifted through hundreds of fonts and designs to find the ones that would best bring this book together, you're the best.

We hope that you, the reader, are inspired by what they've shared.

Contents

Get More (Free) Content

at PrincetonReview.com/guidebooks

As easy as 1·2·3

1 Go to PrincetonReview.com/guidebooks and enter the following ISBN for your book: **9780593517383**

2 Answer a few simple questions to set up an exclusive Princeton Review account. *(If you already have one, you can just log in.)*

3 Enjoy access to your **FREE** content!

Once you've registered, you can...

- Get valuable advice about the college application process, including tips for applying for financial aid

- Use our searchable rankings of *The Best 389 Colleges* to find out more information about your dream school

- Check to see if there have been any corrections or updates to this edition

Need to report a potential **content** issue?

Contact **EditorialSupport@review.com** and include:

- full title of the book
- ISBN
- page number

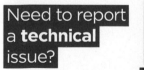 

Need to report a **technical** issue?

Contact **TPRStudentTech@review.com** and provide:

- your full name
- email address used to register the book
- full book title and ISBN
- Operating system (Mac/PC) and browser (Chrome, Firefox, Safari, etc.)

INTRODUCTION

Welcome to *College Essays That Kicked Apps*! Before we turn things over to the 58 students whose contributions made this book possible, here's some information about why this book was compiled, what it contains, and how you can get the most out of it.

Why essays that "kick apps"?

Each year, we hear concerns from the respondents to our College Hopes and Worries Survey about how difficult the college application process can be and how important they've come to find the essay. For schools that have changed some of their admission policies to holistic models and/or test-optional ones or shifted the ways in which they get to know students throughout the pandemic, that essay becomes even more weighted and high stakes. Our desire to ease that pressure led us to compile the *Complete Guide to College Application Essays*, which gave students activities to help them understand their audience, break their writer's block, develop their essay, edit their work, and submit their material.

Still, for many, the essay remains a sort of admissions kryptonite: it renders them at a loss for words, unable to fully express their academic achievements (or superpowers). That's where this book, *College Essays That Kicked Apps*, comes to the rescue. Within these pages, we've put the work of students just like you front and center so you can see exactly what your peers have accomplished—and, by extension, what you, too, are capable of. Each essay read will hopefully demystify the essay-writing process and remind you that instead of being intimidated, you can go out there and kick app! You know how important role models are (some prompts ask you to write about them): here are 58 of them.

While it'd be nice to suddenly wake up with actual comic-book powers, this book will help you identify and hone the real-world powers that are most critical for writing an essay. By reviewing the successful work of fellow students, you can practice and perfect your own techniques as if training alongside them. We emphasize *your own* techniques because, as we hope you'll see from the various essays collected here, there's no one right way to write an essay. After you've read through these essays, if you're looking for additional help reviewing your essay with focused AI editing or with the guidance of one of our experts, visit us online at www.princetonreview.com to explore our professional college admissions options and services.

How were the essays selected?

We wanted the essays within this book to represent all our potential readers, so we considered all essays that were submitted to us by current or former high school students. We did not have any minimum requirements for GPA, nor did we stipulate that students must have been accepted to one of our *Best 389 Colleges* (although that was often the case). Members of our College Admissions Counseling team (www.princetonreview.com/college-admissions/college-counseling) read through the essays— without any personally identifying information— and made their selections based purely on those that they felt showcased a surfeit of variety, creativity, and inspiration. To that end, you'll find essays ranging from Coca-Cola memorabilia to types of handwriting and the Rock 'n' Joe Coffee Bar.

Who wrote these essays?

Each essay opens with a student splash page that provides you with as much personal information as that writer was willing to share. For most of the essays, you'll have at least a first name and last initial, as well as the state from which that essay was submitted. In some cases, we have also included the student's high school to give a little bit of perspective on who this student is and where they've come from outside of the essay itself. Our primary goal was to share these essays with you while also celebrating and recognizing the authors who contributed to this title. At the same time, because many of these essays were deeply personal, we wanted to preserve and respect the privacy of each author where requested.

Where were these essays accepted?

Beneath the information provided by each author is—in almost every case—a list of at least one school that accepted the essay you're about to read. (If one of those schools is highlighted, that's the one that the student told us they were attending.) The college admissions process can sometimes be a bit of a lead-lined black box; our hope is that by sharing this information, you'll have a bit more insight into what has worked in the past and may work again in the future.

What prompts were these essays responding to?

Many of the essays in this book, as is to be expected due to its prevalence in the application process, were responding to Common App prompts from 2022–2023. Those prompts will be the same for the 2023–2024 year, and updates are usually shared around February or March, so if you're planning to submit with the Common App, check their site for more details (www.commonapp.org).

You'll find the specific prompt for each essay printed under the list of schools the student was accepted to. Essays were not chosen based on prompt, but rather on the content of the essay itself, so some topics, like the so-called "generic" prompt ("Share an essay on a topic of your choice…"), may be represented more than others in this book. (As it turns out, this most open-ended of prompts was popular amongst those submitting essays for our consideration.)

The essays in this book are ordered by first name, not prompt, so as to expose readers to as wide a range of styles and responses as possible. However, if you already have a specific prompt in mind and want to find only those essays, please turn to the index on page 215.

How were the essays formatted?

We have chosen a consistent font for all the headers and body text provided to us, but beyond that, we are republishing these essays essentially identically to how these students submitted them to the colleges. While you should strive to edit your own essays multiple times before sending them in, take heart in knowing that in the rare cases of a typo or grammatical error in these submissions, schools looked past them to the heart of the essay and still accepted them.

Why are there annotations?

We are firm believers in active reading: the goal isn't to just read what your peers have written and move on, but to better understand why it may have succeeded and how you might employ similar strategies with your own work. To that end, our team of experts has gotten you started by highlighting with thumbs-up icons some of the lines that caught their attention. They've also explained, at least once per essay, why a particular section worked for them.

What do I need to do?

There's no practice test at the end of this book, no pop-quiz on the contents of these essays. Instead, we're hoping that you'll add your own marks to this book, underlining or highlighting the things that inspire you to move forward with writing your own essay.

The annotations, like the essays themselves, are there to help encourage your own active reading, so that you're pulling as many ideas from each submission as possible and thinking specifically about the language, examples, tones, styles, and literary devices that can help an essay to stand out.

At the bottom of each student intro page, you'll see a thought bubble with the text "IDEAS" written lightly in the background. This is your space to record anything that inspired you about that essay, or where you can brainstorm potential topics, approaches, authorial voices, and more that you might want to try utilizing as you craft your own essay.

Alex D.

Pennsylvania

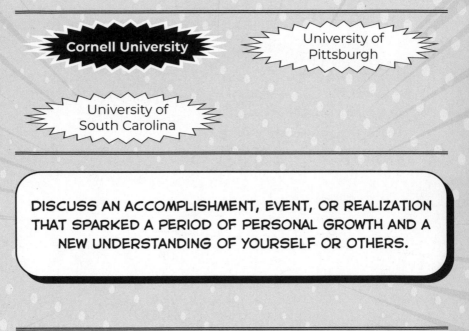

Cornell University

University of Pittsburgh

University of South Carolina

DISCUSS AN ACCOMPLISHMENT, EVENT, OR REALIZATION THAT SPARKED A PERIOD OF PERSONAL GROWTH AND A NEW UNDERSTANDING OF YOURSELF OR OTHERS.

IDEAS

"Not again! Why are you subjecting me to this torture for your own interests?" I complained as I reluctantly spit an exorbitant amount of saliva into a plastic vial. I had just received an Ancestry DNA kit for Christmas because of my mother's fascination with genealogy. When my results indicated that I would not become "follicly-challenged," I practically leapt out of my chair. I couldn't lose that thick head of hair that my family had always so fervently complimented me on. In retrospect, I should not have been happy...I should have been very confused at that moment because both my father and grandfather are bald. Nevertheless, my curiosity had been piqued, and I began sifting through the data until I arrived at my ethnicity analysis. My expectation was that a significant portion of my ethnicity would be Eastern European because my maternal grandfather, whom I affectionately call "Papa", is Polish-Ukrainian. But my results revealed a different story...

As I dove head first into my research, I soon discovered an individual with a very close but unfamiliar DNA match who had already created an elaborate online family tree of her own. Through a detailed analysis of *her* family information, I gradually assembled the pieces of the puzzle. I became captivated by a 1960s black and white photograph of a wild-haired college student from Boston named Ted. I couldn't stop staring at what looked like a picture of my twin! And it couldn't simply be a coincidence that my mom had been born in Boston in the 1960s. How could this be? I was terrified that I had stumbled across a long-hidden, scandalous affair. With my heart racing, I took a chance and fired off

BY INCLUDING A FEW EVOCATIVE LINES IN THE MIDDLE OF THE ESSAY, THE WRITER FURTHER PIQUES THE READER'S INTEREST AND INSPIRES THEM TO READ ON TO LEARN THE ANSWER TO THIS MYSTERY. IT IS CRITICAL TO MAINTAIN MOMENTUM IN AN ESSAY TO KEEP YOUR READER ENGAGED AND INVESTED IN THE STORY.

an email to Ted. Surprisingly, he responded within five minutes and openly admitted, "It is *definitely* possible that I am your biological grandfather." And to my immense relief, he also revealed he had been a sperm donor throughout college to "pick up a little extra cash." A DNA test confirmed that my instinct had been correct.

Intellectually, I felt like Sherlock Holmes with my exciting, newfound knowledge. However, I also began to feel like my mom and I had been deceived by my grandparents, and I was deeply troubled by the complexity of the situation. If I revealed to my grandparents that I had discovered their secret, it would potentially alleviate a fifty-year burden. On the other hand, it could also create tension within my family and possibly damage my special bond with Papa. I suspect that it was a challenging time for my grandparents, and they must have had their own personal reasons for keeping their secret all of these years. As much as I wanted to clear the air, my mom and I agreed that it was not worth the risk of a possible family fallout to share the information.

THIS LINE GETS TO THE HEART OF THE PROMPT. THE WRITER REVEALS THAT THROUGH THIS EXPERIENCE, HE DEVELOPED A NEWFOUND UNDERSTANDING OF HIMSELF.

I eventually came to realize that, as shocking as it was, this new information really did not change my relationship with my Papa in any way. To me, Papa is still my grandfather because the connections that tie us together are much more complex than some strands of DNA. Whether it was Papa queuing up Frank Valli and the 4 Seasons from my phone and cheering me on at my track meets or me helping him fix his computer for the hundredth time, what mattered most was that we had always been there for each other. What began as an attempt to escape the monotony of quarantine flourished into a journey of self-discovery and the realization of the true meaning of family. My unique experience not only sparked my deep interest in genetics, but it also cemented my belief that in our personal lives, as well as in our intellectual pursuits, we have a moral and ethical obligation to consider the impact that our decisions may have on those around us.

Andrea Salas
Santa Monica High School
Santa Monica, CA

Bates College

Bowdoin College

Dartmouth College

University of CA
Berkeley

University of CA
Los Angeles

University of CA
San Diego

University of CA
Santa Barbara

University of CA
Santa Cruz

Williams College

INDICATE A PERSON WHO HAS HAD A SIGNIFICANT INFLUENCE ON YOU, AND DESCRIBE THAT INFLUENCE.

IDEAS

Dear Poppy,

I realize that this letter will not actually be sent to you at Walkley Hill road in Haddam, Connecticut. In fact, it will be sent to the Admissions Office at Dartmouth College. I also know that it has been over two weeks since I received your last letter, and I apologize for not responding sooner. I always have some school-related excuse as to why it has taken me so long to reply, but the truth is, lately it has been hard to write back immediately to my dear grandfather's letters when so much else is pulling my attention away. But once I sit down with pen and paper, I know that thirty minutes later, when I seal the envelope and place it in the mailbox, I will once again be uplifted by feelings of accomplishment and renewed connection to you.

I remember that first letter I sent you ten years ago, thanking you for Christmas money and asking you to "please write back to me, and then I will write back to you, and we can keep a corespondance that way" (that was how I spelled "correspondence" at age six). Those early letters now seem so banal, inevitably beginning with "Dear Poppy, how are you? I am fine." But after a few years, they progressed to "Dear Poppy, I read the most amazing book, *The Count of Monte Cristo.* Have you read it?" I must admit to having told you many commonplace things about myself—my school schedule, the books I am reading, how my sister is doing. but I have also shared with you my most uncommon moments, special moments that seemed removed from time, when I poured out my feelings without concern for what my peers and parents would

RATHER THAN GOING INTO GREAT DETAIL ABOUT HER LETTERS, IN TWO SENTENCES, THE WRITER REVEALS BOTH THE MUNDANE AND THE INSIGHTFUL CONTENT OF THE LETTERS. THIS BREVITY LEAVES THE WRITER ROOM TO EXPAND HER ESSAY INTO OTHER AREAS THAT PROVIDE THE READER WITH MORE CONTEXT.

think. You became the one person with whom I could share feelings back and forth, discussing life's issues, without fear of censure.

When I write to you, I imagine you at your desk reading every word meticulously. Behind you hangs your chalkboard with those Calculus equations that always puzzled me as a child. Now I know that when I next see those equations, I will really understand them! On your desk, a photograph of me, cradled in your arms. When I write to you, I visualize these things and more. Writing to you opens up worlds past and present, yours and mine.

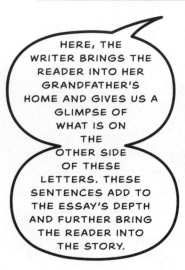

HERE, THE WRITER BRINGS THE READER INTO HER GRANDFATHER'S HOME AND GIVES US A GLIMPSE OF WHAT IS ON THE OTHER SIDE OF THESE LETTERS. THESE SENTENCES ADD TO THE ESSAY'S DEPTH AND FURTHER BRING THE READER INTO THE STORY.

Once I wrote you a letter on a brown paper bag with ripped edges and pretended that I was ship-wrecked, the letter being my only communication with the outside world. In reality, it was only my communication outside my bedroom. There were also the letters written without lifting pen from paper, like the one I wrote when Grandma died. I never worried that I, an adolescent, was trying to console my far wiser grandfather about loss and death. This past August you showed me the folder where you kept all my letters. There at a glance was the Winnie-the-Pooh stationary, the crisp Florentine printed paper, the card of my favorite Alma-Tadema painting at the Getty Museum: the surfaces on which I showed you myself and the depth of my feeling. And all of the letters are addressed to you, Dear Poppy, and signed Love, Andrea, but each is from a different writer at a different moment in her life. Ever changing, yet with you always.

Love,

Andrea

Bella Tancillo

The Pine School
Hobe Sound, Florida

Cornell University

SHARE AN ESSAY ON ANY TOPIC OF YOUR CHOICE. IT CAN BE ONE YOU'VE ALREADY WRITTEN, ONE THAT RESPONDS TO A DIFFERENT PROMPT, OR ONE OF YOUR OWN DESIGN.

IDEAS

After one of my infamously long days, I need to decompress. I wish I could say I read a book or meditate, but the embarrassing truth is that TikTok has me in a chokehold. Video after video, my FYP knows my interests better than some of my closest friends. It knows I work in the restaurant industry, so there are hundreds of crazy customer stories in my recently liked videos. A waitress in Washington vents about patrons who, despite eating their entire meal, want a refund. I'm in Juno Beach, Florida at Matty's Gelato explaining that Peanut Butter Chocolate does contain nuts. It's comforting to be reminded that I'm not the only one facing demanding customers.

It wasn't a surprise for these kinds of videos to show up on my algorithm, but something I didn't expect TikTok to figure out was my fondness for rock tumbling and geology. Essentially, people with National Geographic tumblers search for rocks with potential and put them through grit to reveal the crystal structure underneath. The rocks they find may look ordinary to the untrained eye, but after going through the tumbling process, they turn out to be remarkable. After using increasingly fine grit, the rocks transform. A dull, gray piece of earth may suddenly resemble a tiger's eye, with shining, earth-toned oranges and browns.

BY USING AN ANALOGY, THE WRITER CREATES A COHESIVE THEME IN HER ESSAY. THIS THEMATIC STYLE OF WRITING IS SOPHISTICATED AND REVEALS THE AUTHOR'S STRONG WRITING SKILLS. IT ALSO KEEPS THE READER ENGAGED IN THE STORY.

Interestingly enough, I can find myself relating to those rocks getting tumbled around. I've felt unremarkable before, like in my freshman year. Quiet and afraid of most of my teachers, I faced a steep learning curve. This type of grit was only the tip of the iceberg. More and more was added on through my years, with the arrival of my mother's ex-boyfriend. The amount of stress and pain he caused in my home life, and to my mother, was indescribable. I felt perpetually tumbled around. When I was at my mom's house there were countless times I had to get up and leave at a moment's notice. Eventually, she moved to a boat nearly an hour away from me. I couldn't see her for months at a time.

As all of this was going on, the only thing that kept me from feeling down was thinking of those rocks. I imagine myself as a rock, going through the process of rotating round and round through medium grit. I had to remind myself over and over again, I'll be able to make it through; grit will help me change for the better.

While I needed the money from working, my secret motives were to explore hospitality. The gelato shop was my introduction to what working in service of others could be like. This little mom and pop shop is a place for big groups of families that just finished dinner, and I can't help but watch them and feel like I'm missing something from my own life; a family, unified and having a good time together. Little kids banging on the case's glass, trying to communicate their excitement, only makes me smile. While my own communication skills lacked luster at first, practice made me better. After my nearly two years of working with the gelato and customers, I feel like a manager. When my coworkers panic, either at how to make our classic Gelatowiches or how to ring up a gift card, I am there with my knowledge and advice.

These aren't stories I would generally share with other people, but somehow, TikTok has ears that can hear the unspoken. It's like a little guardian looking after me, even when my own parents cannot. It shows me that I am not alone. I'm less afraid of getting tumbled around now. Having lived a soap opera in the span of a few years, I think the rough moments are just polishing me up to be a better version of myself in the future.

Brandon Molina
Berkeley Preparatory School
Tampa, FL

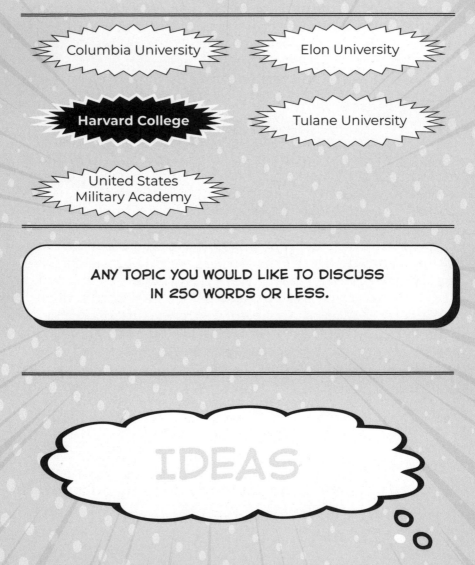

Columbia University

Elon University

Harvard College

Tulane University

United States
Military Academy

ANY TOPIC YOU WOULD LIKE TO DISCUSS
IN 250 WORDS OR LESS.

IDEAS

THE REAL THING

As a seven-year-old, I wrote a personal letter to the president of Coca-Cola, begging for his assistance. Having just returned from a ski trip to Stratton Mountain Vermont, I found myself unable to locate a specific product. At a convenience store on the mountain called "Bear Necessities", my mom bought Coke in eight ounce glass bottles that were reminiscent of those she would buy when she was young (although thicker glass only allowed 6 1/2 oz. of beverage). Whether it was the novelty of the bottles or the nostalgia I knew my mom felt, something made the Coke taste better out of the little glass bottles. I saved the empty container and upon my return home (to Pleasantville, NY at the time), I realized that my local grocery store did not stock these bottles. Neither did the local pharmacy. Neither did the local 7-Eleven nor the one in near-by Chappaqua. In fact, after a day in the White Pages, I realized that the item of my desire was nowhere to be found.

That night at dinner, after telling my parents the story of my day, they suggested that I get some information about the bottles. My mom was a recruiter at the time and furnished me with a telephone number for Coca-Cola. The following day I got a mailing address for the President and CEO, and wrote him a letter. I suppose that not too many seven-year-olds voice their concerns to this man, for I promptly received a response. To my dismay, the letter was an apology. "Unfortunately," it read, "we are unable to provide this product in your region." It began to explain, in very simple terms, that it was not cost effective for Coca-Cola to distribute the product in my densely populated area. His only recourse was to offer me coupons for other Coca-Cola products. For the next two years, I got to sample the bottles on infrequent occasion, whenever we hit the slopes.

My interest in the Coca-Cola Company grew and I began collecting Coke memorabilia, starting with a bank in the shape of a glass Coke bottle, which helped afford later pieces. In sixth grade I was plotting a graph of Coke stock on my America Online account. Also in sixth grade, something great happened: My family moved to our current hometown of Tampa, FL. Here, the eight ounce glass bottles were available in many grocery stores, pharmacies, etcetera. By this time my Coke collection was overtaking my room, and the access to these bottles did not ameliorate the situation. I collected bottles of all ages and editions, some full and some empty.

THIS SENTENCE SUMMARIZES THE CRUX OF THE ESSAY. THE STORY IS ABOUT MUCH MORE THAN A COKE COLLECTION; IT IS ABOUT PERSONAL GROWTH. IT GIVES THE READER INSIGHT INTO THE TRUE MEANING OF THIS COLLECTION AND ADDS DEPTH TO THE STORY.

My collection has meaning that is two-fold. Certainly, a relatively large portion of a seventeen-year life has been devoted to searching, saving, and organizing. However, at a young age, the love that I knew for Coca-Cola taught me lessons about initiative and perseverance that I did not know. Fortunately I learned about these two qualities through a personal interest rather than having to complete an assignment. Of all my Coke products, my Coke-labeled furniture, and my Coke Christmas ornaments, my favorite item is a circa 1920 Coca-Cola glass bottle that was given to me by a friend whose brother found the bottle in a riverbed near Jacksonville, FL. Whenever I look at it, I am reminded of the time when I first began my collection on Stratton Mountain, Vermont.

Brielle Santiago
Indian Hills High School
New Jersey

Arizona State University

Charleston Southern University

Coastal Carolina University

High Point University

West Virginia University

SHARE AN ESSAY ON ANY TOPIC OF YOUR CHOICE. IT CAN BE ONE YOU'VE ALREADY WRITTEN, ONE THAT RESPONDS TO A DIFFERENT PROMPT, OR ONE OF YOUR OWN DESIGN.

IDEAS

I have "Resting Brielle Face" or "RBF." So I am told.

Not a day goes by when a classmate, a coworker, a stranger, or even my parents ask me, "What's wrong, Brielle?" It may seem strange, but my "at rest" facial expression allegedly makes me seem unhappy...or too serious. The simple truth is, however, that once you know me, you know that behind my straight face is an entire girl who is not solely serious but seriously soulful.

I work in the front lobby at Powerhouse Gym, a vibrant and uplifting local gym. I greet customers, assist with membership services, give tours, enroll new clients, and whip up delicious protein shakes. They don't notice if I am too straight-faced, serious, or have something bothering me. The members love stopping by to chat with me. They share their emotional and spiritual stories or update me on their body-building or weight-loss journeys. They show me their before and after photos, photos of their kids, and vacation photos, and one time, Daniel, a member, even showed me his actual police mug shot. I took a double-take. I didn't recognize him. His eyes were dreary, his hair was greasy, and he was at least 100 pounds heavier.

THE WRITER USES DANIEL'S BACKGROUND AS A VEHICLE TO REVEAL HER EMPATHY. ALTHOUGH SHE TELLS DANIEL'S TALE, THE WRITER DOES NOT MAKE THE ESSAY ABOUT HIM. IT IS CRITICAL THAT THE WRITER REMAINS THE FOCAL POINT OF THE STORY.

While showing me his mug shot, Daniel introduced himself. I didn't know what to think initially, so I kept an open mind. Dan explained how he had developed a bad reputation because of the trouble he had gotten into when he was younger. He tragically lost both parents when he was eighteen and lived in a run-down apartment in a bad part of town with his younger brother. They turned to drugs and drug dealing. Ultimately, he and his brother ended up behind bars. I was choked up.

I realized that Dan's past might be hard to understand and that people judged him. But I couldn't understand how they could judge him for *his past*. Looking at him, you would never know what he had been through. Dan was choked up now too. He told me that as time passed and people forgot about him, he entered a very dark place. Fortunately, Dan lifted himself up and started a new beginning. He turned to fitness. Dan expressed how Powerhouse and its positive environment and welcoming staff encouraged him to grow and change as a person. Fitness became his new addiction, and his once-haters slowly became his motivators. We were both teary-eyed. I sensed Dan was in a good place now and was so overwhelmed with happiness for him that I hugged him. He started to cry real tears.

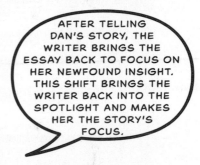

AFTER TELLING DAN'S STORY, THE WRITER BRINGS THE ESSAY BACK TO FOCUS ON HER NEWFOUND INSIGHT. THIS SHIFT BRINGS THE WRITER BACK INTO THE SPOTLIGHT AND MAKES HER THE STORY'S FOCUS.

It was at this moment that I realized who I was. I was "Resting Brielle Face," the warm, welcoming, and non-judgemental face behind The Powerhouse Gym. I go out of my way to greet and check in on our members because I want to hear their stories - successes *and* failures. I want them to know that this gym is *not just a house but a home*. My job is what motivates me, but the people I meet and get to connect with every day are what elevate me. It is the Powerhouse Gym entrance where I feel most alive.

As I consider my future at college, I am excited to make new friends and hear more stories from people of different backgrounds and experiences. Most of all, I look forward to putting myself out there, mask-free. If anyone still has to ask "RBF" if anything is wrong, I'll smile straight-faced and say, "Hey, to anyone asking me what's wrong... NOTHING IS WRONG! EVERYTHING IS AWESOME!"

Bryce Wijesekara

California

University of Chicago

SHARE AN ESSAY ON ANY TOPIC OF YOUR CHOICE.

IDEAS

I'm currently on a journey through the cosmos.

When I plopped down on the couch after a particularly monotonous day of 7th grade, aimlessly traversing through a sea of TV programs, a particular tile appeared that allured my eye. A preview of the show began playing as I hovered over and a vintage radio voice sprung to life- *"The cosmos was all that is, or ever was, or ever will be."* This brief, but pivotal moment was all it took for me to make up my mind. I pressed pause, raced upstairs, and fished out a pencil and notebook from my backpack. Like a man on a mission, I strode back to my living room and began watching Cosmos: A Spacetime Odyssey.

Armed with radiant visuals and the tranquil narration of astrophysicist Neil deDegrasse Tyson, I embarked on a trip through the universe. During my journey, I encountered strange new worlds: worlds of quarks and relativity, of particle physics and dark matter. I knew nothing of these stories, but promised myself that I would return to understand them. As the series progressed, I was fed new nuggets of information that I *had* to investigate further. I researched every word I didn't know, borrowed books from the library every week, and printed out hundreds of pages of articles (much to the dismay of my mom and myself later on).

THESE TWO SENTENCES SUCCINCTLY CONVEY THE PASSING OF TIME AND THE AUTHOR'S INTELLECTUAL GROWTH. THEY KEEP THE ESSAY MOVING AND ALLOW THE READER TO TRANSITION TO A NEW PHASE IN THE WRITER'S EXPLORATION.

I found myself in a poetic pursuit of knowledge—at least to the mind of my middle-school self. However, it wasn't until a few years later that I matured enough to stop, take stock, and ask *why? What truly are the roots of my motivation?* This question differed from those that I had previously asked myself in that they couldn't be answered with empirical data or a logical proof- it simply required you to contemplate, and strive to rationalize the world around you.

 Just as Thomas Kuhn had described paradigm shifts in the context of scientific progress, I experienced a cardinal shift in the way I inquired about our world, ushering in my first tangos with philosophy. My journey opened the door to a world of ideas- from Kant's deontological ethics, to Camus's absurdism, to Eric Fromm's art of loving. While I will never cease to love inquiring about these compelling thinkers, I found myself inextricably drawn towards the intersection between philosophy and the subject that started it all for me one fateful day in 7th grade.

When I stumbled across quantum mechanics, I was met with an insatiable desire to understand. Here was a subject on the frontier of scientific discovery, with massive implications for our entire universe, yet we know nothing about *what it truly means*.

Some contend that philosophizing about the quantum realm is meaningless- fruitless speculation. I found myself greatly at odds with this sentiment—it was vital to convey these ideas with the world. So, I resolved to begin crafting a book—rummaging countless scientific journals, fabricating thought experiments, and contacting field experts to harmonize a whirlwind of ideas into a cohesive piece. By laying the groundwork using physics, and extrapolating those tenets via philosophy, I aspire to make my work accessible to all who inquire.

While it is sincerely gratifying to have devoted many hours into this ongoing endeavor and reflect on the progress I've made, my greatest takeaway was one that humbled me to my core.

The deeper I delved into learning, the more I realized that I truly know nothing. To know in a world where knowledge is imperfect and incomplete makes knowing difficult, especially when you acknowledge your biases and preconceptions. However, in a different frame of reference, this illustrates how knowledge will never cease to grow and evolve. I find solace in the uncertainty of today, fueled by faith in the potency of tomorrow. So, regardless of whether I *know*, I feel limitlessly optimistic of my journey through the cosmos.

Caitlin B.
Ramapo High School
New Jersey

Montclair State University

Syracuse University

University of Delaware

University of Rhode Island

University of Vermont

DISCUSS AN ACCOMPLISHMENT, EVENT, OR REALIZATION THAT SPARKED A PERIOD OF PERSONAL GROWTH AND A NEW UNDERSTANDING OF YOURSELF OR OTHERS.

IDEAS

As my father and I enter the local supermarket, the sliding doors give way to the whoosh of crisp, cool air blended with the waft of warm bakery smells. We are food shopping together, but separate: our Saturday morning ritual. The familiar sounds of squeaky shopping carts and beeping checkout lanes surround us as we part ways. While my father rushes through each aisle to grab what he needs, I prefer taking my time.

I wander through my favorite "healthy aisles" and feel transported. I am in my happy place and my senses come alive. To my right, the shelves are stocked with every nut butter imaginable: almond, peanut, cashew, and even nut-free options like sunflower seed. Across the aisle, the refrigerated wall of vegan proteins, organic eggs, milk, and yogurt never disappoints. I am captivated by the freezers that are brimming with healthy options, including my go-to brand of comfort foods: Amy's Kitchen vegan meals that are quick, easy, yet satiating. Their clean, simple ingredients put my mind at ease when opting for the convenience of frozen food (I am a stressed high school senior, after all). I follow the aisle as it diverts, and I am met by a wall of baking products. Ingredients like "vegan," "organic," and "gluten-free" spark my creativity. My best recipe ideas are born in this aisle, and it never gets old—the adrenaline rush I feel as I scan the sea of Bob's Red Mill products and find exactly what I've been searching for: Oat Flour.

THE WRITER'S HOOK BRINGS THE READER INTO THE ESSAY AND GIVES IT A SENSE OF PLACE. THE READER FEELS THE COOL AIR, SMELLS THE BAKED GOODS, AND IS TRANSPORTED INTO THE SUPERMARKET. THIS TECHNIQUE PULLS THE READER INTO THE STORY AND INSPIRES THEM TO CONTINUE READING.

THE WRITER TRANSITIONS FROM THE GROCERY STORE, WHERE SHE SET THE SCENE, TO THE CRUX OF HER ESSAY; NUTRITION AND WELLNESS. BY SETTING THE SCENE IN PREVIOUS PARAGRAPHS, THE WRITER'S TRANSITION FLOWS SMOOTHLY, BRINGING THE READER INTO THE NEXT PHASE OF THE ESSAY.

Nutrition and wellness have quickly become my source of happiness and creativity. Throughout high school, I developed my passion for clean eating. I experimented with wholesome, plant-based ingredients, learned a lot about food photography, and ultimately was compelled to create a food blog and website. My Instagram account and its companion website have become my outlet for developing and sharing healthy recipes. Having a "space" to engage with and empower like-minded people is a dream. I will never forget the pure joy I felt the first time a follower made my Vegan Funfetti Cupcakes. She posted a picture and tagged me, writing "I decided to make them bite-sized, and they taste like pancakes!

Think pancakes with syrup and rainbow sprinkles . . . a dream!" This inspired and motivated me to continue creating and sharing recipes.

My commitment to plant-based nutrition, intuitive eating practices, and living a life free from diet culture only grows stronger as I continue down this path. While my family might enjoy a nice cut of steak for dinner, I prefer a Dr. Praeger's Heirloom Bean Veggie Burger with a salad of locally grown microgreens, quinoa, avocado, and hummus. Despite my personal desire to eat nutritiously, I do believe all foods can complement a well-balanced diet.

I pick up the bag of oat flour and flip it over. A single ingredient—whole grain oats—brings a smile to my face. Recipe ideas rush into my mind: gluten-free muffin tops, baked oats, refined sugar-free cookies, vegan brownies. My appreciation for nutrition has taught me the beauty of opting for foods with cleaner and fewer ingredients. Food is more than just energy—food is my happiness. I reflect on how lucky I feel to have a creative outlet that allows me to shine and has given me the confidence to be active in a community that shares the same love for food and nutrition as I do.

I toss the oats into my cart and smile as I imagine the rest of my Saturday afternoon baking in the kitchen. I think to myself, "Food is more than my happiness." I embrace this thought. "Food is beautiful."

Carmen Tidwell

Maryland

Rice University

SHARE AN ESSAY ON ANY TOPIC OF YOUR CHOICE.

IDEAS

I start every day the same way. After brushing my teeth, I stumble into the kitchen, eyes half closed, to prepare a breakfast of two eggs; scrambled, two pieces of turkey bacon, a piece of toast, a small cup of coffee with almond milk, and a banana (if we have them). People often inquire about why I chose this specific combination. The answer is that the meal is hearty enough for me to make it to lunchtime without passing out, but it is plain enough not to upset my stomach. It's also pretty cost effective. When I enter the kitchen, the tiles are cold beneath my feet, as the world has yet to wake. The room is filled with an unusual silence, broken by the sizzling of the bacon or the soft rumble of the coffee pot. In the mornings, I'm alone. My mother leaves for work early, so I am left in the company of my tiny poodle, who at this time is begging for scraps. I put on some music to pace myself; usually Norah Jones or Nat King Cole. The ticking of the toaster is like a metronome, setting the tempo for my day. As I gently fold the eggs in the pan, I get a notification on my phone; "reminder: remember to take chicken out of the freezer, meeting at lunch, pick selah up from daycare." Each day is different depending on my family's needs. My family completely relies on my flexibility to function. This often entails watching my four-year-old niece, Selah, taking care of household chores, and making dinner. I make a mental note of the reminder and start assembling my plate. Around this time, I will receive another notification from my Mother. It will say something along the lines of "Good morning! Can you please take out the trash before school? Make sure the kitchen is clean. I'll be home late." I add my Mother's requests to my mental to-do-list, and sit down to eat.

IMAGERY HELPS PAINT A PICTURE IN THE READER'S MIND OF THE STORY AS IT UNFOLDS. WHILE THIS TYPE OF WRITING CAN BE VERY USEFUL IN HOOKING THE READER, IT CAN ALSO BE USED THROUGHOUT THE ESSAY IN ORDER TO KEEP THE READER ENGAGED WITH THE STORY.

The familiarity of each bite soothes me like a weighted blanket. My life is filled to the brim with chaos and spontaneity, so being able to simulate routine is a great comfort to me. Being alone in the mornings gives me a freedom that I often lack. Without people around to ask favors, I am able to be fully in control. This thought process could be a manifestation of my introverted nature, but I think that it's something more. The mornings are my calm before the storm. In the morning I owe nothing, and I'm able to be fully present in the moment.

My mom always tells me "When you are cooking, clean as you go. It makes things easier in the long run." I'd like to believe that I am engaging this idea by slowly chipping away at the tasks that will allow me to build the future of my dreams.

BY BUILDING IN A THEME OF COOKING THROUGHOUT THE ESSAY, THE AUTHOR WEAVES TOGETHER PERSONAL EXPERIENCES THAT DON'T DIRECTLY RELATE TO EACH OTHER IN A COHESIVE WAY.

All throughout high school, I have been tirelessly working towards my goal of attending a 4-year university. What kept me going all these years is a vision of myself studying in a huge university library, or working part time in a bookstore, or exploring the areas surrounding campus with new friends. I strongly believe that college will be the catalyst that will help me to blossom into my fullest self. There are so many niche interests that I have like indigenous agriculture, pottery, and holistic medicine that I could never explore due to financial constraints or lack of time. In addition to acquainting me with people from all walks of life, I hope that college will give me the space to explore these interests as well as my identity. I have faith that college will be a tremendous period of personal growth in my life, and I look forward to it with every ounce of my being. But for now, my eggs are getting cold.

Caroline Habbert

Seven Hills Upper School
Cincinnati, OH

Brown University

Stanford University

University of Michigan

Washington University in St. Louis

Yale University

THERE WAS NO FORMAL ESSAY QUESTION.

IDEAS

This summer I pushed myself to the limit time and time again. Many times when I thought that I could not go any further, I had to rely on all of my inner strength to pull myself through. This summer I spent eight weeks on a bicycle that carried not only me, but all of my worldly possessions for those eight weeks, from Seattle, Washington to Sea Bright, New Jersey. I moved my legs around in constant circles for seven or eight hours a day, every day, all the way from the Pacific to the Atlantic. And at the end of each day, when I was more tired than I could possibly imagine, I set up my tent, rolled out my sleeping bag, and slept until a "mornin' folks" forced its way into my consciousness and told me that it was time to begin the process anew. We encountered crosswinds so strong that we exerted more effort trying to move in a straight line than trying to move forward; swarms of mosquitoes so thick that standing still for more than ten seconds and maintaining enough blood to function were mutually exclusive; huge trucks heading towards us while passing cars on their side of the road, forcing us to abandon the little strip of shoulder we occupied; and, of course, uphill roads than seemed to take forever to crest at the top of the mountain. Despite all of the setbacks and adverse conditions, I made it across the country under my own power. I will probably never again experience anything so amazing as the feeling I had when we first saw water in New Jersey. Getting there had required me to utilize both emotional and physical elements of myself that had never before been tested. I had never before sat on a bicycle seat for 55 days in a row, nor had I ever faced something I wasn't confident I could do. But I did do it. I called upon all of the tenacity,

IN A SINGLE SENTENCE, THE WRITER SUMMARIZES THE CHALLENGES SHE FACED ON HER BIKE TRIP, GIVING THE READER BETTER INSIGHT INTO THE JOURNEY AND BRINGING THE STORY TO LIFE.

persistence, and strength that I have, and I made it.

This is not the first physical challenge I have conquered; my photo albums display mementoes from three other long-distance bike trips. Nor is this the first emotional challenge I have faced. Every week, in fact, I am tested in new ways as a volunteer at a nursing home. During my six years there I have worked with countless residents, but one woman has been a constant. Each time I go, I make it a point to stop by Sarah's room to spend some time alone with her. The first I met her, Sarah was the feisty old lady playing Bingo who explained to me that some of the other women occasionally had a hard time finding the right square. Unfortunately, her spunk did not last much longer. Already 90 when I met her, her health began a slow decline soon after I met her. Most upsetting to me was the fact that her mental facilities were slowly deteriorating. When I first began visiting her, she would challenge my presence on any day other than Sunday. Then, as the days started to blend together, she would realize that it was Sunday when I arrived. Finally, she quit commenting on the days at all. She lost the sparkle that crept into her voice when she talked about her daughter, she stopped telling me about the additions to her photo gallery, and she didn't seem to care about what was going on outside of her room. But she still had enough spirit left to smile every week when I stopped by and ask how I'd been, to listen to me talk about school and my family, the weather and how nice she looked. Until this Sunday, when she didn't recognize me. After I had watched her sleep for a minute, I rubbed her arm and said her name. She slowly opened her eyes and lifted her

HERE, THE WRITER PROVIDES A SIMPLE TRANSITIONAL SENTENCE THAT SEAMLESSLY SHIFTS THE ESSAY'S STORYLINE FROM THE EMOTIONAL CHALLENGES OF HER BIKE TRIP TO HER EXPERIENCE WITH A NURSING HOME RESIDENT. WITHOUT THIS SENTENCE, THE CHANGE IN TOPIC WOULD BE ABRUPT AND THE READER COULD EASILY BE CONFUSED ABOUT THE CONNECTION BETWEEN THE TWO EXPERIENCES.

head off her chest. I waited for the smile and the "Caroline." They didn't come. She closed her eyes and lowered her head again, leaving me squatting by her chair. . .

Watching this transformation has given me my first lesson in the realities of life. Although I am invincible now, I won't always be. Aging is a fatal disease everyone gets if she lives long enough. The nurse I talked to said that she could "go at any time." Time: it is such a relative thing. When I was on my bike this summer, the hour that it took to go twelve miles sometimes seemed like it would never end. The two months that I was gone seemed to last forever. But I can still remember the day that I met Sarah six years ago as vividly as if it were yesterday. And it doesn't seem fair that Sarah's life, long in terms of human time but short in relation to the world, will soon be a memory too.

Caroline Mellor

Walt Whitman High School
Bethesda, MD

Bard College

Reed College

DESCRIBE A PERSONAL STRUGGLE.

IDEAS

BALANCING THE SEE-SAW

 "Beat her up," one of them shrieked; referring to me, while the four of them pounded their fists into their hands on the sidewalk corner. I had merely suggested that we run faster, but my cross country teammates' response demonstrated that they didn't agree. Although they were entirely kidding about the violence, such a strong statement was quite frustrating.

For me, running isn't just a stress reliever; it has become a way of life. I look forward to escaping into the looming trees of the Capital Crescent Trail, for this place has more worth to me than just being able to escape into it. Deemed the cross country team's "den mother," I'm always ready to take someone home, help them stretch, listen to her trials and tribulations during a long run, and even organize our annual running camp trip to Vermont. But in this instance, they wanted to do less than what was required to accomplish our best and my not allowing the weaker choice to be made, just didn't settle well with them.

After an awkward silence, we began our daily run with the temporary resolution to decide on the eventual pace as we went. We darted past the middle school and across the neighborhoods, with only casual comments, such as announcing when one spotted a yellow car as we made our way into downtown Bethesda. The first red light we came to changed too fast, leaving us with no time to move to a solution on our work ethic conflict. We continued past the commercial glitter at every store, and came to the intersection of Green Twig Road and Wisconsin Avenue. Then my twinkle of laughter at a street name turned into an explosion of giggles at our absurd conflict. I then exclaimed, "girls, where are we going?" Laura, Rachel, and Kate looked at me as if I belonged in the "abnormal" section of my Psychology textbook, while the only action Becca could muster was to raise her hands to her ears and hiss at me. Then I added, "ah, no, not our route... I meant the point of being here, are you guys... feeling okay—enough for a smudge more?" As the concern echoed through my stern voice, I received understanding nods from my fellow runners as we pressed on through the buzz of traffic to finish our run at the harder pace I had requested.

We did make out daily water stop at a local coffee shop, where they always seem to feel sorry for us, as when we come struggling in, they respond quickly with our cups of water. When we returned from our run, we may all have been on "runner's highs," but the discontented sentiments seemed to have disappeared on their own. We had completed a sweltering nine mile run, and now as we strode to the same sidewalk corner, words of "thanks, the run felt amazing," came from my teammates.

I knew that tomorrow I would be able to physically and mentally take myself farther, while today I had compromised just enough to keep the team bonded. Even though I may have sacrificed a portion of my own success for the team, that part will be returned in the form of the team's success and happiness. That afternoon I felt marvelous myself and almost enjoyed being the "bad guy." It is important to listen to those around you, but only while eavesdropping on what you are thinking yourself.

WITH THIS SENTENCE, THE WRITER REVEALS THAT THE ESSAY IS ABOUT MORE THAN A NINE MILE RUN. IT GIVES THE READER INSIGHT INTO HER CHARACTER AND ALLOWS US TO UNDERSTAND HER PRIORITIES.

Christina Anne Ellinger

Dana Hall School

Cornell University

THERE WAS NO FORMAL ESSAY QUESTION.

IDEAS

Ancient things speak to me. The stories they tell fascinate me. I feel a personal connection to people, places, and objects from before modern civilization; this is my passion. I first felt it as a twelve-year-old in Pompeii—the ruins immediately captured me as I envisioned people going about their daily lives, unaware of the disaster that would soon strike. Plaster casts of the bodies left behind especially caught my attention and made the experience more personal. This fascination with history has inspired my choice of academic interests and my summer activities.

My freshman Western Civilizations class exposed me to other civilizations, and English class introduced me to the Odyssey. I fell in love with history and the classical civilizations all over again. Western Civ quickly became my favorite subject and the teacher became my mentor and academic advisor. When I lobbied successfully for a family trip to Greece, she gave me extra readings and suggestions for places to add to our itinerary.

AT THE END OF HER INTRODUCTION, THE WRITER PREVIEWS HER ESSAY'S TOPICS. THE READER NOW KNOWS THAT THE STORY WILL INCLUDE BOTH ACADEMIC INTERESTS AND SUMMER ACTIVITIES. WITHOUT THIS SENTENCE, THE TRANSITION TO THE WRITER'S WESTERN CIVILIZATION CLASS WOULD SEEM ABRUPT AND OFF TOPIC.

In Greece I once again could close my eyes and imagine the Ancients thousands of years ago standing right where I was. At the Marathon Tumulus I could envision the Athenian soldiers celebrating their victory over the Persians and honoring the 192 dead. Climbing the hill at Delphi, I imagined the Greeks taking those same steps after long journeys from distant cities to consult the Oracles and basing critical decisions on the cryptic messages they received. At Mycenae I could feel the presence of Bronze Age people passing through the Lion Gate. When I climbed down the tunnel steps into the well, it seemed that the only thing separating me from a girl going to get water during a siege was my flashlight and a few thousand years.

With these experiences, I became interested in how we know so much about these cultures. Ancient literature gives us firsthand accounts; however, the study of archaeology caught my attention as the key to reconnecting with the past. No longer content with just visiting tourist sites, I decided I would literally have to get my hands dirty to understand history the way I did in the well at Mycenae.

I found a dig the August after my sophomore year that would allow an inexperienced sixteen-year-old student to join. It was a program just for teenagers at a Roman fort along the River Tyne in England. The fort was built in the second century AD to supply the forces along Hadrian's Wall. Just as the Romans had carefully built walls to create structures, I was carefully taking them down to understand how they had been made and why. I was thrilled by the idea that I was contributing to knowledge of the Romans in Britain by digging up turf blocks.

My love for archaeology increased throughout the next year as I kept up with current news, and I found another dig for my junior year summer—a Roman fort again, but this time on the Spanish island of Menorca. The field school at Sanisera was more sophisticated—all college students, except me. I was given what proved to be the most interesting task: excavating a garbage pit. Part of the challenge was finding the original purpose of the pit. Was it a cistern? A well? Or maybe a cooling pit for amphora? I had lunchtime debates with my professor (in Spanish) about exactly how the shape was related to its purpose. Although the hours and temperature were much more grueling than in England, I willingly woke up at 5:00 A.M. every morning to excavate my own little pit.

 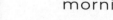

While I am most interested in the Greeks and Romans, I can feel this same connection to more recent history. In my job as a library assistant at the Massachusetts Historical Society I handled important items such as John Adams' boyhood diary and an annotated draft of the Constitution. Both of these artifacts made history seem so much closer and more real to me because they were physical evidence I could hold in my hands. Even more recent than Revolutionary America is South African apartheid. On a community service trip to Soweto, I had the opportunity to meet Antoinette Pieterson Sithole and hear her talk about her brother Hector's death. Walking up the street with the locals, I could feel the world-changing events of June, 1976 all around me. It made me wonder if the people involved knew just how important they were to history. It was exactly the same feeling I got in Pompeii four years earlier.

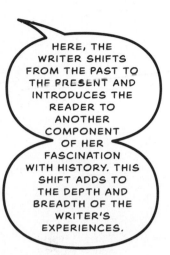

HERE, THE WRITER SHIFTS FROM THE PAST TO THE PRESENT AND INTRODUCES THE READER TO ANOTHER COMPONENT OF HER FASCINATION WITH HISTORY. THIS SHIFT ADDS TO THE DEPTH AND BREADTH OF THE WRITER'S EXPERIENCES.

Although I do not yet know where my passion for classical civilizations will lead me, I am sure my connection to the period will be lifelong. I am not sure where my college studies will take me; perhaps I will become a teacher, or maybe I will become a professional archaeologist. Either way, it is already an interesting journey and I cannot wait to continue it in college.

Claire M.

Greensboro, North Carolina

Georgetown University

AS GEORGETOWN IS A DIVERSE COMMUNITY, THE ADMISSIONS COMMITTEE WOULD LIKE TO KNOW MORE ABOUT YOU IN YOUR OWN WORDS. PLEASE SUBMIT A BRIEF ESSAY, EITHER PERSONAL OR CREATIVE, WHICH YOU FEEL BEST DESCRIBES YOU.

IDEAS

Have you ever heard that little voice inside your head, articulating your thoughts? Mine takes form through penned letters on a piece of paper. The loops and lines have a quiet yet powerful voice, speaking in a way I do only after thorough consideration. From silly notes about things I need to remember to time-intensive papers during AP exams, my thoughts don't just live in my head: they have a vacation home within a notebook or on a sticky note. They are eager to leave my brain, representing me out in the world.

A SEEMINGLY SIMPLE FACT ABOUT HANDWRITING REVEALS DEEPER ASPECTS OF THE AUTHOR'S PERSONALITY AND DEMONSTRATES THAT A COLLEGE ESSAY DOESN'T NEED TO FOCUS ON A LARGE, MONUMENTAL, OR LIFE-CHANGING EVENT TO BE IMPACTFUL.

Penmanship is a person on paper. Mine appears as thoughts do in my mind, neat and concise, yet the size does not convey the importance. I often sit in class, taking my time to organize my thoughts, allowing my more gregarious classmates the chance to speak up first until I have my ideas in order. When my words emerge, they are eloquent and strong. My handwriting is my outlet, my second brain. It is small as I am introverted, it is neat as I am meticulous. I like to think that it's recognizable to teachers as authentically me, not because they find it difficult to read like I've been told many times.

Despite being small, my handwriting is powerful. My steadfast energy toward an idea makes it fun to write, elaborating my ideas on paper until they are complete. With the unpopular opinion that Document Based Questions are fun and my inherent nature to avoid writing over the vertical red lines on notebook paper at all costs, I've been called crazy. But my penmanship is far from it, growing in neat lines with semicolons and commas and inflection, evoking a sense of confidence. When I speak, after careful thought, I'm proud of my observations. Those tiny little penned words string together to form success, change opinions, bring people together, and argue a point, leaving their influence on others.

I take time writing each word in uniform sizes and marking them out if I'm not satisfied with the angles and curves of the letters. My brain moves the same way, tweaking and reworking ideas until they are finally up to my standards. Letters and precision come slowly in the world of a perfectionist. Instead of being crippled from fear by minute details and multi-step plans, I am overcome with a sense of excitement. The occasional cursive lines and flourishes are my penmanship's way of conveying emotion. Its style matches my curiosity and my drive, gradually flowing faster and faster from the tip of my pen as I embellish my ideas, eager to give my thoughts permanence yet still leaving room to expand on them.

People like to tell me to make my handwriting bigger, darker, but then it wouldn't reflect me accurately. Bold lines through sentences are evidence of my progress. I am always thinking everything through with precision and care, willing to rewrite and reword until I'm satisfied. My handwriting shows my ideas, my doubts, and my determination. Erasing a word is erasing one of my many starting points toward a brilliant idea. My writing looks most natural in pen; after all, most pencils have poor erasers that smudge and leave my words messy like jumbled thoughts.

In no way did I choose my handwriting: it chose me. The style of my sentences and letters remains constant as the words sit stubbornly on the paper's blue lines, unwilling to change themselves for someone else just as I am true to myself. Since middle school, my handwriting has forced teachers to put on their reading glasses to see into my mind. I've apologized for those little letters, but not their meaning. My pride and confidence is reflected in my writing, illuminated by my minute yet mighty penmanship. Aren't you glad you get to read my essay in 12 point font?

ADDING A QUIPPY QUESTION TO THE END OF THE ESSAY SHARES MORE ABOUT THE WRITER'S PERSONALITY AND TONE, BRINGING THEIR VOICE TO LIFE FOR THE READER.

Clara Marie Cassan

Lycée Francais of New York

Connecticut College

Dickinson College

McGill University

New York University

St. Andrews University

Wesleyan University

DESCRIBE AN EXPERIENCE THAT CHANGED YOUR LIFE PERSPECTIVE AND HELPED YOU DISCOVER SOMETHING ABOUT YOURSELF.

IDEAS

I remember the moment when I accepted what I love to do. Until then, I had always been the late bloomer, the searcher. Now that I come to think of it, one of my passions had always been right in front of my eyes, just waiting to be grasped. Yet, I never believed that what I already knew about myself was enough, and I stubbornly assumed there was something better out there. I was in dogged pursuit of an elusive goal, on the lookout for a passion, hunting, scratching the dirt off all things that could be potential interests. But nothing really came of it until I stopped looking. It was this past summer at Columbia University's writing program. I had decided to spend three weeks writing, something I had always enjoyed, but had mistakenly considered a tool, not a goal. The point of the classes was to introduce us to all types of writing, and we studied everything from poetry to prose and screenwriting.

One of the assignments was to write a play. The day before it was due, I turned my awareness to all likely characters in daily life, scrutinizing every person I could possibly bump into on my way back home—yes, I am the creep that stares at you on the subway. I tried to capture each moment of brief action on the streets as an inspiration for my assignment. When I sat down to my computer that night, my writing came to life. I didn't experience the familiar writer's block I had felt with other school projects. The dialogues between my characters came so easily; it was as if I had overheard them somewhere, and the scene was as clear as a place I had lived in for years. I felt like I was remembering something I had never known, and creating felt spontaneous and natural.

She falls heavily on her chair, rolls her shoulders, and hunches her back brutally. She drops her bag next to her and scratches the end of her nose. She looks around as she...It was an obsession. I had to transform everything I saw into some sort of mental screenplay. Each song I'd hear turned itself into a picture even if I didn't want it to. It's been like that ever since. Writing the play had helped me solve the mystery of what it was I loved to do, but, of course, it was only the beginning of a long process I have barely begun today. I decided to start teaching myself. As often as I can, I read the screenplay as soon as I see a movie.

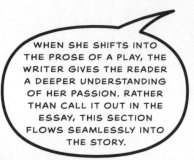

WHEN SHE SHIFTS INTO THE PROSE OF A PLAY, THE WRITER GIVES THE READER A DEEPER UNDERSTANDING OF HER PASSION. RATHER THAN CALL IT OUT IN THE ESSAY, THIS SECTION FLOWS SEAMLESSLY INTO THE STORY.

My curiosity has been more demanding ever since I wrote that first play. Writing has enabled me to find inspiration even in things I abhor, like the cacophony of New York City streets at rush hour. I just find a way to make it mine and turn it into writing. Now I understand that all I learn, see and hear can help in different ways. Realizing this has made me more implicated in my environment. I am anchored in the life I create everyday in the sense that I realized how much more fulfilling it is when I devote myself entirely to the places I am in, and the people around me. Because being observant comes from participation and full attention. Recognizing my love for writing has helped me proffer, but has also been gratifying. My world offers me much more intensity, helping my creativity's activeness. I am no longer searching relentlessly, but keeping my senses alert. Watching with commitment makes every detail matter.

THE ESSAY COMES FULL CIRCLE WHEN THE WRITER REFERENCES HER SEARCH FOR A PASSION. SHE OPENED HER ESSAY WITH THIS SEARCH AND NOW SHE CLOSES WITH THE REVELATION THAT SHE IS NO LONGER SEARCHING. THIS REFERENCE ADDS CONTINUITY TO THE ESSAY'S THEME AND PROVIDES THE STORY WITH A RESOLUTION.

Daniel Freeman

North Farmington High School
Farmington Hills, MI

Yale University

> APPLICANTS ARE TO WRITE ABOUT AN ACTIVITY
> THAT WAS IMPORTANT TO THEM.

IDEAS

THE CONQUEST

It was a crisp, clear June day in Rocky Mountain National Park, a few miles outside of Estes Park, Colorado. Before me stood an imposing sight: Estes Cone. With a peak at twelve thousand feet above sea level and a base at eight thousand, this mountain would be a challenge for any hiker. I was no hiker; I was an unathletic, awkward 15-year-old boy. Nonetheless, I loaded my pack with salami, pita, and water and set forth.

> THE WRITER USES HIS INTRODUCTION TO SET THE STORY'S SCENE. THE READER SEES THE MOUNTAIN FROM THE WRITER'S PERSPECTIVE AND IS TRANSPORTED INTO THE MOUNTAINS OF COLORADO. WE ARE READY TO EXPERIENCE THE HIKE WITH THE WRITER.

At first the going was easy. I knew we had to ascend four thousand feet before reaching the peak, and as we passed the fourth of five mile-markers, I questioned whether we had gained more than fifteen hundred. After lunch my trip's supervisor explained the situation. The next mile included almost three thousand feet of vertical gain. We would split into two groups: one would go quickly, the other would be allowed breaks. The fast group would see the top and the slow one would be forced to turn back when they met the others coming down. I decided then that no chunk of rock could conquer me, and so I set forth with the fast group.

The pace was grueling. My muscles screamed out for rest, and I began to regret that I had chosen to audition for the musical instead of trying out for the tennis team. As we pushed forward, the angle of elevation increased from twenty degrees, to thirty, to nearly forty. I fell further and further behind until I was told that I should simply wait for the slow group to catch up and continue with them. I curtly responded that I would be fine and proceeded onward. Pain tore through my legs as I pulled my body weight over each rock. The back of the group flittered in and out of my view, pulling me forward with only dim hopes of success.

Time wore on, and pain faded into numbness. Each foot followed the other in a grim succession. The trees thinned with the increasing altitude, and the peak grew nearer. Suddenly I heard my friend Dan holler down, "Hurry up man, you've just about made it, and we're sick of waiting for you!" My vigor restored, I pushed on quicker than before until I broke through the tree line. A bald, craggy expanse of rock surrounded me. The others were waiting, cameras in a pile, in preparation for a group shot at the summit. In one final act of endurance, I pulled myself over the top to join the others in triumph. My climb was complete.

As I looked down from that peak upon the miniaturized ranger station and the surrounding vistas, I received two things. One would shape my leisure time for the remainder of high school – a love of hiking. Whenever I get the chance, I escape from suburbia and enter the wilds. Since that fateful summer I have hiked in three countries: through the heat of Israel's Judean Desert, over the rocky cliffs of Canada's Lake Superior Provincial Park, and throughout the forests of my native Michigan's many state parks. I now am a hiker. Even more importantly, I was given confidence. Physical limitations and the limitations that others place on me no longer deter me from setting and reaching my goals. Life is my mountain, and no rock-strewn face will keep me from reaching the summit.

BY USING THE MOUNTAIN AS A METAPHOR FOR HIS LIFE, THE WRITER REVEALS THE ESSAY'S TRUE MEANING.

Daniel Mejia
Lawrence High School
Lawrenceville, NJ

Amherst College

Georgetown University

Harvard College

Rutgers University

Tufts University

THERE WAS NO FORMAL ESSAY QUESTION.

IDEAS

Beep, beep, beep. My alarm goes off at 5:30 AM. I dart outside in my oversized t-shirt and pajama pants to bring in the newspapers as the rain pours out of the sky onto the freshly printed papers. The daily morning pressure has begun—I must deliver the papers by 6:30! Why did it have to rain today? I get onto my bicycle and prepare

WITH HIS LIVELY AND CREATIVE INTRODUCTION, THE WRITER ENGAGES THE READER AND BRINGS US INTO HIS STORY. WE ARE INSPIRED TO CONTINUE READING TO SEE WHERE THIS ESSAY GOES.

to enter the dark, misty, morning ... Whoa, I almost rammed into a stray trashcan in the road. I swerve to the left to avoid a giant puddle. Okay, my first house is a porch customer. I get off my bike and run through the grass up to my customer's porch twenty feet away, but on the way I step in dog poop. I'm just going to have to move on—a paper boy's got to do what a paper boy's got to do! I begin to shiver with mud on my clothes and water leaking into my old sneakers. There are only five papers left. After another grueling ten minutes I'm finally done! I begin to walk inside the house to dry off, and of course it stops raining at that moment.

Why do I keep this job, a job that requires getting up in the wee hours of the morning to deliver newspapers to demanding and unsympathetic customers? There are the obvious reasons, such as for making money, gaining responsibility, learning how to run a business, and meeting many new people. But, well, there's another reason that I don't like to admit to the "guys;" I also do it for a girl. Not just any girl, but rather a girl whose very presence has changed my outlook on the world and allowed me to escape the typical high school goal of popularity.

Fast forward six months, and I have finally saved up enough money to buy a used 1996 Nissan Maxima and to take this girl, Megan, to New York City's Tavern on the Green, the restaurant of her dreams. (Trust me, it's a restaurant that has very "undreamy" prices.) Megan is bursting with excitement as we walk through Central Park to get to Tavern. It's her sweet sixteen birthday. I put my arm around her and point out the "bright stars in the sky"; she giggles, but gives me those sarcastic eyes. She knows I'm overdoing it. Finally we go in and have a great time despite my reminder that she does not need to order the most expensive entrée. The night is followed by my surprising her with ice-skating under the Christmas tree at Rockefeller Center. Personally I do not get too many thrills from the night's activities. Nonetheless, her ecstatic smiling eyes at the end of the night prove that at least this morning's paper delivery was worth it. I secretly get my own joy driving us off in my new used Maxima.

IN THIS PARAGRAPH, THE WRITER'S TOPIC SHIFTS, BUT HE MAINTAINS HIS DESCRIPTIVE STORY-TELLING, KEEPING THE READER INVESTED IN THE ESSAY.

Danny Finch

Pascack Valley Regional High School
New Jersey

Boston College

Notre Dame

Rutgers University

Villanova University

REFLECT ON A TIME WHEN YOU QUESTIONED OR CHALLENGED A BELIEF OR IDEA. WHAT PROMPTED YOUR THINKING? WHAT WAS THE OUTCOME?

IDEAS

There is a major concern I have about the concept of heaven; if I'm to be in a supposedly idyllic place for all eternity, won't I get bored? If there are no problems to solve and no work to do up there, how will I pass the time? It's hard for me to imagine not having goals to work towards, and it raises many questions for me—namely, how will I spend my time in heaven?

BY POSING A UNIQUE SET OF QUESTIONS ABOUT THE TOPIC OF HEAVEN, THE WRITER HAS HOOKED THE READER AND LEAVES THEM WANTING TO LEARN MORE ABOUT THE AUTHOR'S THEORY OF HEAVEN. THERE ARE MANY WAYS TO HOOK A READER, AND ASKING A THOUGHT-PROVOKING QUESTION THAT TIES INTO YOUR ESSAY IS SURE TO DO THE TRICK.

Will I attend mass every Sunday and watch football games on weekends? Are there fantasy football leagues in heaven? If so, will I be able to retain my position as commissioner? I already struggle for half the year without football; what would it be like for all eternity? I don't want to find out!

Are holidays celebrated in heaven? Will I be able to continue my family's long-held Thanksgiving and Christmas traditions? Growing up, my mother never had big family Thanksgivings because most of her extended family lives in Puerto Rico. For this reason, she now loves hosting large gatherings for Thanksgiving, as do I. And what of Christmas? Will I still awake Christmas morning to the sounds of my favorite holiday tunes and the delightful aroma of cinnamon rolls, croissants, and biscuits? Will I continue to celebrate the tradition of *El Día de Los Reyes*—the day the three kings brought gifts to baby Jesus? I cherish the holiday season and hold these customs near to my heart. My perfect world would have to include them.

I'm a problem-solver. Give me a problem, and I'll spend hours or days finding the solution. In heaven, I'll have a lot of time to solve problems. But do people have jobs in heaven? I don't know what the rules are up there, but if I were permitted to influence life on earth, I surely would. I would start with global warming, which won't be easy and cannot be handled alone. I would assemble the greatest minds—from Socrates to Einstein. If permitted, we would whisper into the ears of world leaders, subtly swaying their policies—or, we could take a *Christmas Carol* approach. Three angels could come down from heaven and visit each world leader. The first would explain how the temperature has risen in the last hundred years. The second would reveal the horrible effects of climate change such as the Australian wildfires and rising sea levels. The third angel would provide a window into the future of the planet if we fail to take immediate action.

Next, I would turn my attention to aiding those living without basic civil liberties under oppressive governments such as China and North Korea. Progress will not come quickly, so thousands of angels would have to come down to earth to impart the virtues of democracy amongst the people. Then, through civil disobedience and nonviolent protest, change would occur. I suspect teamwork would make a difference in heaven as it does on earth.

As a child, I hoped that heaven would be akin to a long vacation to Disney World—the "happiest place on earth." I dreamed of living there for all eternity—riding all the rides and eating anything I wanted. However, I have realized that this paradisiacal existence would soon become mundane; true heaven would have challenging problems for me to help resolve. Maybe I could become a guardian angel, sitting on people's shoulders and steering them towards making good choices. That would surely keep me busy in heaven. Ideally, I'd play fantasy football, continue my family traditions, and help solve small-scale and global issues on Earth. With so much to do, I would be anything but bored.

David Averbach

Sprague High School
Salem, Oregon

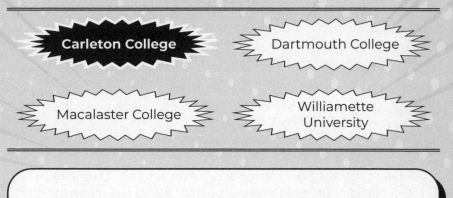

Carleton College

Dartmouth College

Macalaster College

Williamette University

CHOOSE ANYTHING YOU WANT TO WRITE ABOUT.

IDEAS

CLEANING YOUR ROOM CAN CHANGE YOUR LIFE

Recently, during a futile attempt at cleaning my eternally messy room, I tripped over the leg of a chair and fell sprawling to the floor. As I lifted my head, I found that I was at eye level with the very bottom shelf of my bookcase. One book on it caught my eye—a book I had last read in eighth grade. I pulled the book out and began to read....

I read of a world where the written word is forbidden, where books and other printed material have been banned for decades. Without the printed word, intellectual life withers and debate dies. In the absence of debate there are no disagreements. In this dystopia, all are equal because no one excels and mediocrity rules. All are therefore happy. On the surface, the system seems to work.

THE WRITER BEGINS HIS CONCISE, YET THOROUGH, SUMMARY OF THE BOOK. THIS APPROACH IS UNUSUAL, BUT WORKS IN THIS ESSAY.

Enter Guy Montag. Guy is a fireman; that is, his job is burning books. He enjoys his job, for he knows he is making the world a safer and happier place. He is a perfect product of the system...until he meets Clarisse.

Clarisse and her family are misfits. In Guy's hyperaccelerated world, they still enjoy walking. In his world, questions are discouraged, because asking questions is part of the process of discovery. Clarisse is expelled from school for asking questions. She has a natural curiosity about others; in her words, "I just want to figure out who [people] are and what they want and where they're going." Perhaps the most profound question in the book is Clarisse's simple query to Guy: "Are you happy?"

As he ponders this question, Guy realizes the fallacy behind the "equality" he fosters. By destroying books, he forces people (including himself) to give up their individuality and ability for independent thought. They become dependent on the system, expecting everything to be handed to them on a plate.

> AFTER HIS SUMMARY, THE WRITER TELLS US WHY THE BOOK CAPTIVATED HIM. HAD HE NOT PROVIDED US WITH THE SUMMARY, THE WRITER'S LESSONS WOULD BE DISJOINTED AND CONFUSING. NOW THE TRANSITION FROM BOOK TO LESSONS LEARNED IS SMOOTH.

What did I learn from this book? I learned from the frenetic pace of Guy's world to slow down and take time to enjoy life. I learned from Clarisse's curiosity that there is nothing wrong with asking questions. I have always been an inquisitive person, but since first reading this book, I have become even more inquisitive about the world around me. Finally, I learned the incredible power of knowledge. Knowledge bestows the power to create or destroy. It enables us to judge and to choose. The ability to make decisions is what makes each of us so different and interesting.

For me, reading this book was a life-changing experience. I often pause and ask myself: "What knowledge have you gained today? What power has that knowledge given you? How has it made you different?" One additional difference reading that book made to me was the realization that books and especially their contents need to be protected in order to avoid mediocrity. And thanks to Ray Bradbury, I now know that *Fahrenheit 451* is the temperature at which book paper burns.

Diana Schofield

Ravenscroft
Raleigh, NC

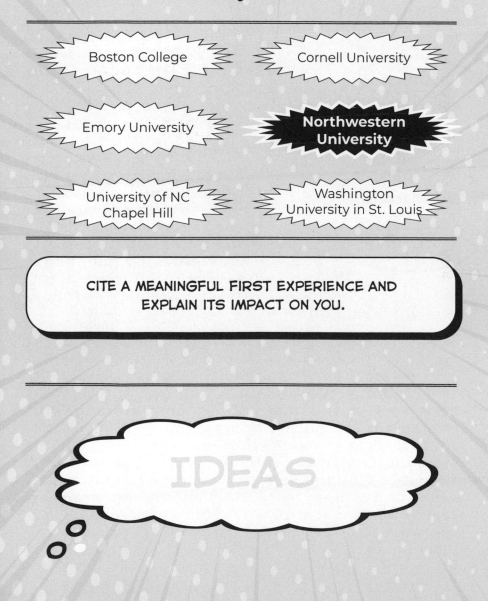

Boston College

Cornell University

Emory University

Northwestern University

University of NC Chapel Hill

Washington University in St. Louis

CITE A MEANINGFUL FIRST EXPERIENCE AND EXPLAIN ITS IMPACT ON YOU.

IDEAS

I greatly appreciate the concept of taking a *siesta* in the afternoon. I love the fact that the salad comes after the main course, and the cars are all the size of Volkswagen beetles. Olive oil really can accompany any meal. You can't go anywhere without seeing a duomo or a fresco. Punctuality is not a necessity of life. No one in Italy ever seems to be in a rush, because there is no time.

THE WRITER USES A BRIEF QUOTATION TO ENHANCE HER ESSAY AND SUMMARIZE HER EXPERIENCE IN ITALY. QUOTATIONS SHOULD BE USED SPARINGLY, AND SHOULD ADD TO THE READER'S UNDERSTANDING OF THE STORY.

E.M. Forster wrote, "The traveler who has gone to Italy to study the tactile values of Giotto, or the corruption of the Papacy, may return remembering nothing but the blue sky and the men and women who live under it." Such was my experience as I, a student of music, spent a month in Spoleto, Italy this past summer. I originally applied for a spot in the Spoleto Study Abroad program in order to play the violin, study opera, history, and learn Italian. But what I came away with was the influence of the Italian culture, which will follow me wherever I go.

As I lugged my overweight, eighty-pound suitcase (nicknamed "The Big Mama") down a narrow cobblestone alley, I wiped the sweat-smeared makeup from my forehead and worried about what the lack of air conditioning and overwhelming humidity was going to do to me. And no email? Nevertheless, I couldn't wait to start classes, begin rehearsals, and get out into the city. I couldn't seem to get over my American ways of rushing from one activity to another; "exhausted" became my only response to the typical Italian greeting "Come stai?" As I wearily walked to class one morning, I noticed this incredible view overlooking most of Spoleto.

I stopped dead in my tracks and studied the fog settling over the tiled roofs of modest stone houses. Laundry lines hung from window to window like vines. This was not the Italy of the Olive Garden and Parmesan cheese commercials. This *was Italy*. Why had I not noticed this magnificent site before? I took a picture, and every time I passed that spot, I paused to study the amazing world below me. My American schedules and routines were discarded, along with my makeup and hairdryer. I slowed down, took many scenic

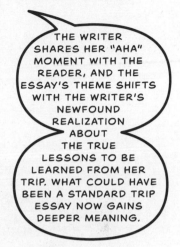

THE WRITER SHARES HER "AHA" MOMENT WITH THE READER, AND THE ESSAY'S THEME SHIFTS WITH THE WRITER'S NEWFOUND REALIZATION ABOUT THE TRUE LESSONS TO BE LEARNED FROM HER TRIP. WHAT COULD HAVE BEEN A STANDARD TRIP ESSAY NOW GAINS DEEPER MEANING.

routes, began sampling new flavors of gelato, and trying out my nascent Italian skills on vendors in the piazzas. I could spend literally hours sitting in cafes chatting with friends, and in a very "Lost Generation" style, writing in my journal. Living in Italy for a month is more than eating the food, purchasing postcards, and attempting to decipher the language, it is living the life and the culture. In that month I became an inhabitant of the country, an Italian by my lifestyle and mindset. When I physically returned to the States, my thoughts were in Spoleto, Florence, Siena and in other beautiful cities. As I readjusted to life in Raleigh, North Carolina, I never lost my Italian flair. I discovered that Italy is not only a place, but also a state of mind.

Elizabeth Jeffers Orr

Littleton High School
Littleton, CO

- Bates College
- Kalamazoo College
- **Kenyon College**
- Lewis & Clark College
- Oberlin College
- University of Denver
- University of Puget Sound

WRITE ON A TOPIC OF YOUR CHOICE.

IDEAS

Beaches are meant to be rocky and gray. The ocean is meant to be deep blue and frigidly cold. You have to jump in because getting in step by step is intolerable. Everyone else's white sand and turquoise blue fantasies mean nothing to me. I know only the whitecaps and fog, along with the trees and cliffs, that surround the beach of my memories. Every recollection I have, of any summer, involves Skillings, my family's summer home on the coast of Maine. The wooden walls of that one-hundred year old house contain remnants of not only my childhood, but also the echoes of three generations of my family, who all vacationed there.

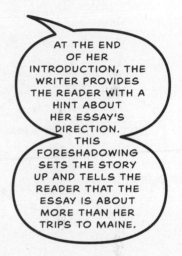

AT THE END OF HER INTRODUCTION, THE WRITER PROVIDES THE READER WITH A HINT ABOUT HER ESSAY'S DIRECTION. THIS FORESHADOWING SETS THE STORY UP AND TELLS THE READER THAT THE ESSAY IS ABOUT MORE THAN HER TRIPS TO MAINE.

It is easy to forget that I am part of this extended family. I am at least ten years younger than the rest of my generation; all of my cousins already have kids, some of them approaching middle age. I live in Denver, approximately fifteen states away from any other family member. Out of the myriad of genetic possibilities, I inherited my mother's hair, skin, and eye colors, making me a dark-skinned brunette, a rarity in this family of pale, blue-eyed red heads. Age, location, and appearance all loosen the obvious ties to my family.

Sometimes I question what we have in common, but there is a connection. My dad and uncles used to swim in this ocean when they spent their childhood summers at Skillings. Their names are carved into the sixty-year-old furniture. Here I share toys and books with my cousins, who have already moved on to adulthood, and with my father, who doesn't remember leaving them behind. They slept in the room I sleep in now, just as my cousin Becky did before me. She left a pair of sandals here seven years ago. I borrow them sometimes, just as I borrow the raincoat my aunt Louise used to wear. Everyone who comes to stay at Skillings leaves something behind; Becky's shoes, Louise's coat, my dad's copy of <u>Just So Stories</u>. I can picture some future niece or nephew of mine wearing the same goggles I've worn, diving head first into tidal pools to stare at the same starfish with which I've been transfixed.

At the end of every vacation, as our car pulls out of the driveway, I get my last glimpse of the deep blue water, and I cry. Only at Skillings do I feel like part of my extended family. Although most of them are older and far away, I know that, just as I do, they revisit their history here. Skillings encases the memories and belongings of my family, pieces of our lives, saving them for later, for others. Unlike me, the older members of my family no longer cry when they leave, but I know they did once. Maybe some day, once I'm older, I will stop, too. Until then, I will leave the remains of tears behind to mingle with those of my family, who all are at home amongst the rocks and fog.

THIS SENTENCE SUMMARIZES THE CRUX OF THE ESSAY. THE STORY'S CONTENT LEADS THE READER TO THIS MOMENT, AND WE UNDERSTAND WHY THE WRITER'S SUMMERS IN MAINE ARE SO IMPORTANT.

Ellison Ward

The Nightingale-Bamford School
New York, NY

Brown University

Connecticut College

Duke University

John Hopkins University

Princeton University

William & Mary

EVALUATE A SIGNIFICANT EXPERIENCE, ACHIEVEMENT, OR RISK THAT YOU HAVE TAKEN AND ITS IMPACT ON YOU.

IDEAS

THE WRITER'S HOOK GRABS THE READER'S ATTENTION AND ENCOURAGES THEM TO READ THE ESSAY. A GOOD HOOK IS A CRITICAL MEANS OF ENGAGING YOUR READER.

So I'm sitting on my couch, wrapped in a blanket that I have somehow wrestled from my sister, enthralled by the electrifying activities taking place before me. The movie is *Outbreak*, and our star, Dustin Hoffman, is in the middle of a standoff with his superior officer, Donald Sutherland. Their argument centers on a certain town in California, contaminated with a certain deadly yet suddenly curable virus, and a plane carrying a chemical agent that will wipe out the entire population of the aforementioned town. "No!" my sister shrieks. "Don't drop the bomb!" As the plane veers out over the ocean, the missile flies into the crystal clear waters and creates an immense, mushroom-shaped wave. "All right!" shouts my family, as out of the jubilee rises my tearful cry, "Wait! What about the marine life?!"

All right, so this is an overly dramatic version of the actual events, but the gist is the same. My bizarre attachment to the fictional fish is largely a product of my summer; I worked for eight weeks in the Coral Lab of the New York Aquarium on Coney Island. I'll admit that my interest in the Natural Sciences was pretty general; I thought corals were beautiful, and I had fond memories of childhood trips to the Aquarium every time I visited my aunt and uncle in Virginia. I was thrilled to be working at the lab, but when you came right down to it, one truth remained: I had no idea what I was doing. No amount of ninth grade biology (or tenth grade chemistry or eleventh grade physics, for that matter) could have prepared me for the intricacies of the filtration system in a room full of corals being used for research projects or the manual dexterity required by the micropipeting process. But by the time August rolled around, not only had I mastered the fine art of maintaining a number of different filters and the rather painstaking procedure of micropipeting, but I had figured out what it is that has always drawn me to the sciences. Everyone I met, no matter how grating, overbearing, or bossy he might have been, could be reduced by the mere sight of a tank to an awed silence. And most that I met were not in any way grating, overbearing, or bossy. In fact, they were enthusiastic, dedicated, and friendly to anyone interested in their field to the point of annoyance. And they are just who I want to be.

The funny thing about this whole essay is that I don't even want to be a marine biologist. What I really want to study are the Earth Sciences, but the specifics are not important. I learned this summer what it is to be passionate about what you are doing, to have an unchecked enthusiasm for even the dirtiest aspects of your work. To spend your life in the quest for knowledge that could make the world a better place may sound like a lofty goal, but when it's a real possibility, it's utterly amazing. Like any profession there are twists and turns,

HERE, THE WRITER RESPONDS TO THE PROMPT BY SUMMARIZING HER SUMMER JOB'S IMPACT ON HER. IT IS CRITICAL THAT EVERY ESSAY ADDRESSES ITS PROMPT.

opportunities for frustration, disappointment, and conflict, but everyone in that lab knows he is doing something he can be proud of and that might help the world better understand how we can save our planet. Now that I have seen the kind of passion and love with which these people work at their jobs, I would never settle for anything less.

Emily Allen

Henry M. Gunn High School
Palo Alto, CA

Georgetown University

University of CA Berkeley

University of CA Los Angeles

University of CA San Diego

University of Southern California

SHARE AN ESSAY ON ANY TOPIC OF YOUR CHOICE.

IDEAS

My summer partner and I stood, watching the truck rattle away, leaving us alone by a rural Bolivian farm. We turned to each other, matching expressions clear on our faces: What have I gotten myself into? Did I ever think volunteering for eight weeks in a Spanish-speaking community would build my language fluency and sense of responsibility? *Claro que sí.*

Last summer I participated in *Amigos de las Américas*. In *Amigos*, two teens stay with host families in a Latin American country and work on projects chosen by the local community. Eight months of training sessions led up to the summer experience; I attended fifteen evening meetings, five Saturday workshops, and three retreats. At the same time I raised over $4000 by selling grapefruit, oranges, and poinsettias and by writing letters asking friends and family to sponsor me. I also engineered an additional $2000 grant from my dad's company to help with scholarships in my chapter of *Amigos*. I enjoyed preparing and giving presentations to parents and fellow trainees, especially because I got to improvise a cohesive talk out of a bare outline of information.

I put Bolivia as my first choice, so I was pleased that I got to go there. My Bolivian community chose two projects for my partner and me: facilitate the completion of the community building—a doorless, windowless, two-room project abandoned several years earlier—and hold English classes for local kids at the school. The latter project succeeded because the students showed an eagerness to learn. With classes held for an hour, six days a week, we soon discovered the difficulty of creating new lessons and activities. In addition, the lessons had to be adaptable for an age range of six to sixteen and a group size range of three to forty-three. When we had enough high school students to make a separate class, I would take them into another classroom to help them with their English homework and questions. When I had difficulty eliciting requests for what they wanted to learn, I would spontaneously use my background in drama to create a lesson such as touching each body part as I named them or creating family trees to remember the words for various relations. The younger students especially enjoyed the games we taught them, and I occasionally overheard a spirited game of Perrito (my loose translation of Red Rover) being played during school recess. One time, before class, the school gatekeeper (who never complained about having to come back in the evenings to re-open the school after-hours for our classes) brought a set of dominoes to me and asked me to translate the English playing instructions. I felt thrilled that I could provide that small service for him.

Our other project, the community building, took longer to show progress. We had a hard time getting workers to come to the building site to use the materials we had bought. We would visit one town leader's home, and after making polite conversation we would finally ask for and receive a promise to send workers the next day. When no one showed up to work with us, we would look for the man we had talked to, only to discover he had left for the day and wouldn't be back until dark. This happened several times with different leaders, so we finally held a town meeting, with our field supervisor present, to explain the urgency of finishing the construction before we left in three weeks. Apparently the meeting worked, because three to six workers started showing up every day at the site. When we left, the doors and windows were installed and the interior walls were painted.

THIS SENTENCE REVEALS THE WRITER'S CREATIVE APPROACH TO PROBLEM SOLVING, A SKILL THAT IS KEY TO SUCCESS IN COLLEGE.

I expected that my summer with Amigos would be more fulfilling than, for example, a week-long "mission trip" to Mexico with a youth group because the personal accomplishment would be clear. I would wake myself up, set my own schedule, and take care of the details of completing projects. I saw myself taking on a comparable level of responsibility for projects at college and in a future business setting. As it turned out, I found no such clarity about who was responsible for events. Perhaps, if I had pushed harder, the community would have worked on the building faster. However, that might have led to a lack of community responsibility and sustainable interest in and maintenance of the building after my partner and I left. The community played such a large role in the work that I soon realized I could take care of my end of things, but only encourage them to work on their parts. Once they got going, it was exciting to see their growing enthusiasm extend to new plans to add on a kitchen, bathroom, and patio to the existing building. When I left, workers had already dug the hole for the bathroom, bought the supplies for the kitchen, and arranged to continue the shifts of workers. When I look back at my summer, I can admit that I didn't do everything single-handedly. Nonetheless, I still take pride in my participation in the whole community effort. Even without the expected results, my experience will help me when I work on projects in the future. I also have come away with more confidence in my adaptability: if a truck dropped me off in a rural village today, I know I could move past any initial uncertainties to explore new ways of understanding my world.

IN THIS FINAL SENTENCE, THE WRITER SHARES HOW THE LESSONS SHE LEARNED IN BOLIVIA WILL STAY WITH HER. IT IS IMPORTANT FOR AN ESSAY TO SHOW HOW AN EXPERIENCE CAN IMPACT YOUR FUTURE.

Emma Fricke

Belmont High School
Belmont, MA

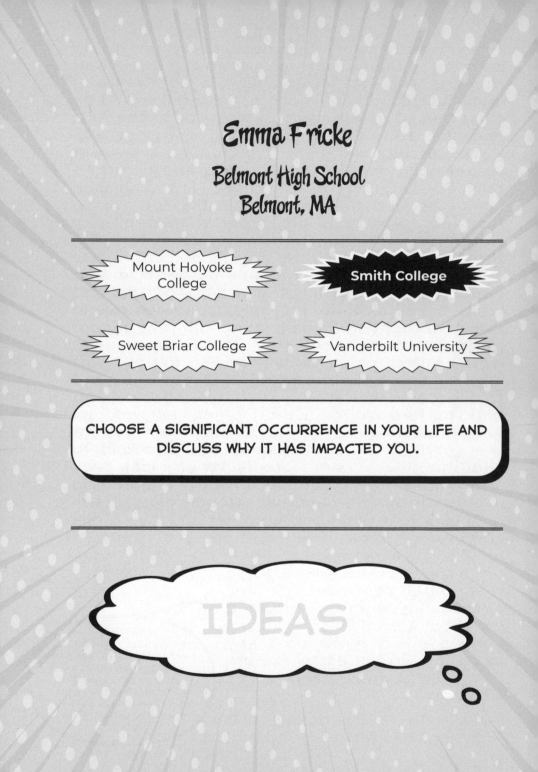

Mount Holyoke College

Smith College

Sweet Briar College

Vanderbilt University

CHOOSE A SIGNIFICANT OCCURRENCE IN YOUR LIFE AND DISCUSS WHY IT HAS IMPACTED YOU.

IDEAS

What first comes to mind when the words sing-a-longs, radio shows and art projects are listed together? For my brother and I, these words have a special meaning. For us, they mean to load up our suitcases with every single "important clothing item" and fill our back-packs with tapes, art materials and any other fun items that we deem "necessary" for yet another Road Trip.

BY POSING A QUESTION AS HER HOOK, THE WRITER ENGAGES THE READER'S IMAGINATION AND ENCOURAGES THEM TO READ ON AND LEARN THE ANSWER.

For as long as I can remember, my family has been throwing gear into the car and heading off on adventures. My brother and I have always been in charge of packing our own bags and bringing things to keep us entertained. Usually, we don't need many material items. We pool our imaginations to invent games, sing songs, and play bingo. We also do back scratching, head massaging, and feet fighting. The two of us always bond no matter how feisty we have been during the weeks before. Together, we fall into our "road trip mode" of cooperation the second we hit the highways.

I am by no means saying that every road trip we have taken has been perfectly pleasant. Once, my brother, who was three months old at the time, screamed all the way from Texas to Missouri. When I was two and my brother was not yet one we moved from Texas to Massachusetts. On the last leg of the journey in Connecticut, my father came down with the chicken pox. I am told that when I was four on a trip to Alabama, I sang the same song over and over for an hour. At that point I calmly announced, "Let's turn the record over!" And for the next hour I sang a new song. Another time, when I was in eighth grade and I thought hard rock was the coolest. I made my family listen to it all the way from Boston to Florida. My brother and I have also gone through "creative" stages. On our annual road trip to Missouri, we decorated all the windows of our car with beeswax clay. "Hey Mom," we exclaimed, "when it melts on the windows it looks just like stained glass!" Another time we made glitter paintings. We called the glitter "magic dragon dust." When we arrived at our campsite for the night, the mystical "dragon dust" covered our entire bodies, our seats and the floor (and about 1% of it was on its actual designated spot, the paper). The dragon dust lingered for years in the car. On a road trip, mechanical difficulties are bound to happen. En-route to Minnesota, our alternator belt fell off along the highway. We exited quickly but couldn't find a gas station anywhere. Luckily, straight-ahead was K-Mart. Rejuvenated with hope, my brother, my best friend and I ran in, asking every sales clerk around if they could find us a new alternator belt for the car. "No" was the answer. Picture us: a family (plus one) sitting on the curb eating carrots at K-Mart next to a smoking and smelly car. We didn't give up, though. Eventually, my dad found a tow-truck service to take him to a gas station so he could buy a new belt. Pretty soon, we were back on the road again singing our hearts out.

As the years have progressed, our Road Trips have changed significantly. Now we have three drivers instead of two and we all can agree on music (well, sort of). My brother has become a professional backseat driver and we can go for longer than one exit without having to stop for a bathroom break. Lately though, my family has begun taking road trips with my father's brother and his family. They have four children ages two, four, seven and nine. Now my brother and I are the designated babysitters instead of the babysittees. They have a van and so my brother and I sit with kids piled on each lap and entertain. Last year, while driving from Alabama to Florida to visit our grandparents, we successively rapped every child's song that we could think of; rap, apparently, is now the cool music of choice (not hard rock, like I used to think). We also have refined our talent of making up stories "No, I want a scary bunny story, not a funny alligator story," and have learned the gift of patience.

This gift of patience is invaluable. In order to succeed in what I love to do, working with young children; patience is something that I have to draw upon often. When I am ready to throw up my hands in desperation while babysitting or working in the church nursery, I remember how my parents dealt with my brother and me throughout the years of Road Trips. Smiling from this, I roll up my sleeves and whip out some glitter and paper or begin to sing the songs that I remember from my childhood. My parents have taught me that children are a gift and their creativity and outlook on life is something that should never be suppressed or overlooked. Now that I am a senior in high school, I am sad to think that my road trip days with my family are almost finished. Hopefully, college will be one big Road Trip where I will use the important aspects of creativity, compromise and overcoming obstacles. I will always know how to enjoy life even though what is presented to me may not be "magic dragon dust."

> AFTER SETTING THE SCENE AND ENGAGING THE READER WITH STORIES, THE WRITER DIRECTLY ADDRESSES THE POINT POSED IN THE PROMPT.

Emma Teutonico

Staten Island Technical High School
New York

Fordham University

Fairfield University

George Washington University

Honors College at CUNY Hunter

Lafayette College

Northeastern University

Siena College

DISCUSS AN ACCOMPLISHMENT, EVENT, OR REALIZATION THAT SPARKED A PERIOD OF PERSONAL GROWTH AND A NEW UNDERSTANDING OF YOURSELF OR OTHERS.

IDEAS

"YAY, Lily! You're a BIG girl now!" I cheered as she finished her two-year well visit. Lily beamed at me with a big smile and pointed to the babies in her mommy's tummy. She was soon going to be a big sister. The energy and excitement in the exam room were palpable.

Since the eighth grade, I have fostered a deep and genuine interest in biology, anatomy, and bioscience. It was the summer before my sophomore year in high school, and the pandemic was in full swing. Extracurriculars were canceled, and with nothing to fill my days after school, I decided to reach out to my local pediatrician's office and offer to work as a volunteer. Dr. Bucca welcomed me with open arms, as she was *my* pediatrician and knew me personally. I began as a volunteer on Saturdays. I assisted Dr. Bucca and the office staff by greeting families, taking patients' temperatures, and leading them to the exam rooms. I would end the day by deep cleaning and disinfecting the exam rooms, the front office, and the waiting room. As the year progressed, I developed a strong bond with Dr. Bucca. She suggested I come more often and shadow her. I was excited to assume more responsibilities simply because I loved being there.

For the next year, I followed Dr. Bucca as she instructed me and became immersed in the patient visits, check-ups, chart-reading, and note-taking. More importantly, however, I formed relationships with the patients and families I had fast come to know. The time I spent in the office with Dr. Bucca was truly meaningful. I took pride in our young patients' achievements and accomplishments, whether they grew an inch or more, showed proper weight gain, or overcame short or long-lasting illnesses. However, the most profound realization for me was that there was a "flip side" to pediatrics. Not

THESE SENTENCES GET TO THE CRUX OF THE PROMPT. THE WRITER SETS THE SCENE TO GIVE THE READER CONTEXT, THEN REVEALS HER NEW UNDERSTANDING OF PEDIATRICS.

everything was positive. While there were easy conversations, there were hard conversations. Observing Dr. Bucca as she delivered negative or even ambiguous diagnoses or prognoses were some of the most challenging conversations I have witnessed. I still recall the looks of fear, confusion, and despair as families digested unwanted news. But then, there are the conversations you cannot fathom. The ones that shape you...

Two months ago, while at the office, I was excited to see that Lily's family was on the schedule. When they arrived, Dr. Bucca pulled me aside to remind me that the family had been expecting twins, but due to complications at birth, their son passed shortly afterward. I froze, unable to process this news. I wondered how Dr. Bucca felt as she personally went out to reception and escorted the family into the exam room. I was disoriented about which to focus on - the life of their newborn daughter, their son's death, the mom's mental health, or Dr. Bucca and the conversation. I felt so small and insignificant. But then, Lily tugged at me, smiling, and pointed to her new sister asleep in the infant carrier, and *THAT was my AHA moment. That day, my eyes opened wide and my heart wider.*

BY SHARING HER "AHA" MOMENT, THE WRITER REINFORCES HER RESPONSE TO THE PROMPT.

Throughout high school, it has been primarily the sciences and mathematics courses that have driven and challenged me, ultimately confirming my passion for becoming involved in research and medicine. My experiences with Dr. Bucca and her patients over the last two years have inspired me to pursue my focus on pediatrics. Preparing for college, I am excited to continue my rigorous study and curiosity. I imagine how I will work and collaborate with peers to make great strides in medicine and research so that together, we can have a significant impact not only on patients but also humanity. *While lessons in academics have enabled me, it is the more significant lessons in resilience, hope, and empathy that have empowered me.*

Faith Nancy Lin

Arlington High School
Riverside, CA

University of CA
Berkeley

University of CA
Los Angeles

University of CA
San Diego

Yale University

WRITE ON A TOPIC OF YOUR CHOICE.

IDEAS

I hope that Yale University has a large supply of water. When I say this I am not referring to a love for the nearby Atlantic Ocean or for the aquatic sciences. My infatuation with water springs from a different source. The water that I am most concerned with is that which washes over me when I take a shower. I am the type of person who spends much time in the bathroom, and while some individuals may find showering to be a trivial and even unnecessary part of their routines, I believe that my hygiene habits have played a role in developing many of my personal characteristics.

I refuse to go to bed without taking a shower. Though showering can be time-consuming, I am unable to forsake this beloved activity. Over the years it has trained me in the area of commitment, equipping me to excel in my academic studies. My high school record attests to the fact that I devote a wholehearted effort to whatever I do. Past trials have taught me that if I neglect either my daily shower or my scholastic studies, I will only experience a feeling of uncleanliness.

THE WRITER CONNECTS THE BASIC ACT OF SHOWERING TO CRITICAL COMPONENTS OF HER LIFE. SOMETHING AS SIMPLE AS A SHOWER CAN HOLD A DEEP MEANING AND INSPIRE AN ESSAY.

I am not the only person in the house who showers. Thus, I have been required to learn how to work around my family's schedules, sharpening my skills of time-management in the process. These skills benefit many areas of my life. Last year Arlington High School was able to take home the Envirothon state championship because of the team members' abilities to manage their time. As a team co-captain, it was especially important that I learn to arrange my schedule. I have always been able to allot time for showering, no matter how busy I may be, and in the same way, I managed to attend Envirothon practices while remaining involved in church activities and focused on my academic studies.

Oftentimes I must be the last one to shower to ensure that everyone in my family receives hot water. Showering teaches me the ways of self-sacrifice so that I put others' needs before my own. It has encouraged me to make other sacrifices. Volunteering at the hospital means that I am unable to spend my Saturday afternoons with friends. Playing piano for Sunday service means that I must spend hours practicing. My hectic schedule sometimes leaves me little time for myself.

Showering is important to me because it sets apart a time for relaxation and reflection. The bathroom provides the perfect atmosphere for pondering since there is little chance that I will be interrupted, and the rushing water has the ability to stimulate my thoughts with its gentle sound. Within the tiled walls I am able to draw life lessons from the commonplace events of each day. In numerous ways, showering connects to the life I lead outside of the bathroom. Showering allows me to take time to simply contemplate, and I would like to think that I finish each shower a more thoughtful and self-aware individual.

> IN HER CONCLUDING SENTENCE, THE WRITER REINFORCES THE DEEPER MEANING OF HER SHOWERS. THIS REINFORCEMENT ADDS STRENGTH TO THE STORY.

Gaurav P. Patel

The Walker School
Marietta, GA

Dartmouth College

University of Pennsylvania

FIRST EXPERIENCES CAN BE DEFINING. CITE A FIRST EXPERIENCE THAT YOU HAVE HAD AND EXPLAIN ITS IMPACT ON YOU.

IDEAS

Here I was in Hemingway's "moveable feast," yet unfortunately I was without a feast of my liking in Paris during Oxbridge Academic's L'Académie de Paris on the program's French Language Scholarship and the National French Honor Society's Travel Award. In the world's culinary capital, I, a true francophile who cannot get enough of the French culture, could not find anything to eat. Surely, the croque monsieur or even les escargots tempted the taste buds of the over one-hundred other participants in the program; but my taste buds seemed to cringe at the sight, god forbid the smells, of such foods. However, I somehow survived on les sandwich and by my fascination of France and what else she had to offer.

PERSONIFICATION, SUCH AS THE MENTION OF THE WRITER'S TASTE BUDS CRINGING, IS ONE STRATEGY TO BRING THE WRITING TO LIFE FOR THE READER. INCORPORATING FIGURATIVE LANGUAGE INTO AN ESSAY IS AN EXCELLENT WAY TO ELEVATE WRITING.

My classes Littérature française and Medicine at L'Académie unmasked the educational merits that often lie hidden behind façades for the "traditional" visitors of Paris. Classes began at 9:00 a.m. after a French breakfast and ended at 12:00 p.m., when students traversed the Parisian streets to grab a sandwich and enjoy lunch in the Luxembourg Gardens or in the gardens of the Rodin Museum. Minor classes began at 2:00 p.m., but the city became a teacher's aide, a type of three-dimensional video. Studying literature and fashioning my own poems in a café where Hemingway used to frequent or creating my own literary "salon" at la Mosquée became reality during class. The beauty and the scintillation of the French language came to life even more so for me. I never ceased to be enthralled, for I was finally immersed in the culture, the language, and the tradition of my academic passion in life: French.

The whole city transformed into a massive university; there was always something to learn outside of classes. Attempting to speak French with a native or ordering lunch in French became a unique type of erudition. While studying abroad, I not only received a stable background with lively teachers in my classes, I also began to experience French life— I was a Parisian for one full month (or at least I tried to be).

In Paris, I never had a dull moment. Whether it was a walk to the Eiffel Tower or a short journey to the nearby Versailles or a candle-light stroll in and around Vaux-le-Vicomte, I never tired. Having a cappuccino with my newfound friends at a café as we watched others briskly walking by on the Champs-Elysées or travelling on the Métro became adventures. The French culture offers a city and a country where the joy of life is present all around.

Nevertheless, I had to leave my utopia. On my last stroll around Paris and in the Luxembourg Gardens on the morning of my departure, I came to realize that I had had an extraordinary experience that many will never savor. Learning French amongst les français was a dream that I had finally fulfilled, and it is a something that I crave yet again— without the food if possible.

Ivan Russell

Institute for Collaborative Education
New York

Cornell University

DISCUSS AN ACCOMPLISHMENT, EVENT, OR REALIZATION THAT SPARKED A PERIOD OF PERSONAL GROWTH AND A NEW UNDERSTANDING OF YOURSELF OR OTHERS.

IDEAS

The slick clay slides through my fingers, spinning as a separate entity as I force it to the center of the wheel. It's centered when it doesn't wobble or fight me. When it spins so flawlessly it appears unmoving. If I pull up the walls and form a shape before it's centered, it collapses. If I make adjustments too quickly, the walls cave.

Pottery is an art that demands stability. You must be patient when forming a pot; your hands need unwavering steadiness, and movements must be measured. Perhaps that's why I'm drawn to it. Growing up with ADHD, it was a struggle to organize my time and focus. I bounced around friend groups and activities without finding my place. I wasn't aware of it, but what I craved was structure. It was similar when my parents divorced. I was in first grade, and suddenly I had two houses, two lives, and an awkward feeling of staying with one parent or the other. Nowhere did I feel like anything was stable or complete about me.

THE STABILITY THAT POTTERY REQUIRES BECOMES A METAPHOR FOR THE STABILITY THE WRITER CRAVES IN HIS LIFE.

THE WRITER WEAVES THE POTTERY THEME THROUGHOUT THE ESSAY, USING IT AS A SPRINGBOARD FOR OTHER TOPICS. THIS THEME ADDS TO THE ESSAY'S FLOW.

Pottery has been my constant. I've been practicing it since I was five. Every Saturday I walked to a studio owned by the same woman for half a century. The rituals of cleaning up and unloading kilns happened the same way, week after week and year after year. I loved the familiarity of her and her studio. Dusty pieces from decades earlier were scattered in the back, and the environment stayed constant as I grew.

It wasn't until the pandemic that I found an academic subject with as much power to fascinate me as pottery. When the world locked down, I drew inward. Summer was starting and I felt lost. A quantum mechanics class I was excited about was cancelled. I needed a way to stop myself from stagnating, and realized that if I wanted a solid education I alone would be responsible. I started teaching myself advanced math online. Later that summer, I tried a college-level astrophysics course. Immediately, everything changed. I couldn't do the difficult math, but the concept enthralled me. I took notes on everything. I gained momentum, and soon was ready to start Calculus and teach myself AP Physics 1. While studying mechanics, the scale at which I was learning expanded dramatically. All of a sudden, I was solving problems about piston engines and rockets orbiting our planet.

Equations felt reliable, absolute. Trigonometric formulas specifically have a centering, stabilizing quality. I didn't immediately see connections between physics and pottery. Soon I realized I could describe the circular motion of the wheel with physics. The forces at play, the inward acceleration and the relationship between diameter and structure. Physics began shaping my mind the way my hands shape clay.

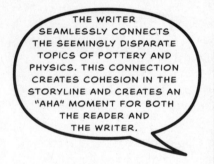

THE WRITER SEAMLESSLY CONNECTS THE SEEMINGLY DISPARATE TOPICS OF POTTERY AND PHYSICS. THIS CONNECTION CREATES COHESION IN THE STORYLINE AND CREATES AN "AHA" MOMENT FOR BOTH THE READER AND THE WRITER.

A deeper understanding of physics changed how I threw pots. I created ambitious and complex forms: spherical moon jars, delicately spouted vessels, even urns for my cat's ashes. I better understood the motion of the wheel, knowing where the clay was too thin or thick and whether to keep pulling or compress the walls. Pottery was something I relied on, but suddenly I wasn't just throwing bigger and taller objects, but experimenting with glazes, oxides, techniques of carving and slipping; an entirely new art was unlocked.

Physics has given me confidence and clarity of mind. Solving problems and working through formulas has turned my eyes into computers, breaking down things I see into numbers and equations. Seeing a simple balloon will have my brain scribbling formulas for buoyancy and the ideal gas law on the backs of my eyelids. It has made me more intuitive, like I've been given the secret code of the universe, and with it the ability to understand everything that ever happened and ever will. It's crazy to think I came this far in just over a year. But, as Newton's first law entails, I will only keep advancing.

Jalen Riad

St. Louis Priory School
Missouri

Davidson College

DAVIDSON ENCOURAGES STUDENTS TO EXPLORE CURIOSITIES IN AND OUT OF THE CLASSROOM. WHAT IS A TOPIC, ACTIVITY OR IDEA THAT EXCITES YOU? TELL US WHY. EXAMPLES MAY INCLUDE HOBBIES, BOOKS, INTERACTIONS, MUSIC, PODCASTS, MOVIES, ETC. (250-300 WORDS)

IDEAS

Although most of us drive or walk on roads every single day, most people don't think about them too much. For a while, I didn't either, until, seemingly out of the blue, I started carefully looking at the roads where I live. I became so interested in road layout and planning that I began scouring over any research I could get my hands on. The first thing I really began to focus on was road hierarchy, which classifies roads according to their size and purpose, and organizes how they should interact with each other. Although I had driven on all kinds of roads throughout my life, I never thought about the differences between freeways, arterial roads, collectors, and local roads. As I got deeper into road design, I learned about subconscious ways in which city planners force you to drive more carefully, whether it is putting tall trees on either side of the road to slow you down, or focusing your attention on pedestrians by putting traffic signals low and near pedestrian crossings. I found that intersections are the centers of creativity for road designers. Intersections are an unusual part of road planning, as they require vehicles to be able to stop, switch roads, or continue onwards, all while being safe with the rest of the cars on the road and moving traffic efficiently. This has resulted in beautiful intersections such as the diverging diamond interchange, the quintuple roundabout in Swindon, and the displaced left turn continuous flow intersection. The ways in which city planners design these intersections to eliminate cross-traffic turns is very interesting to me, and although I know my knowledge of road and intersection design won't help me much in the future, I will keep researching and giving my friends uninvited lessons in city planning.

FOCUSING ON A UNIQUE INTEREST UNRELATED TO WHAT THE AUTHOR PLANS TO STUDY DEMONSTRATES THAT THEIR CURIOSITY IS PIQUED BY EVERYDAY OCCURRENCES AND THAT THEY ENJOY RESEARCHING AND LEARNING ABOUT A VARIETY OF TOPICS, A SKILLSET VALUED BY COLLEGES.

John Newell

Saint Louis Priory School
Missouri

Vanderbilt University

SHARE AN ESSAY TOPIC OF YOUR CHOICE.

IDEAS

Snoozing and punctuality are arch enemies, and I am an addictive snoozer. Punctuality is one way to show you care. I need both, so each morning I sacrifice some sleep, having set my alarm just a bit earlier. Thus, I allow myself to snooze *and* be timely—all for a small price. This ritual of combining two contrary forces has led me to search for more *and,* and less *or.*

Often, we are called to choose between two opposing ideas, pulling us to one side or the other. But a successful tennis player finds the equilibrium between power *and* control. A successful student learns from teachers *and* students. Neither the right nor the left has a monopoly on good ideas and policies. To me, success involves *and,* not *or.*

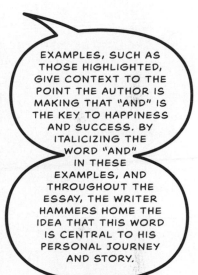

EXAMPLES, SUCH AS THOSE HIGHLIGHTED, GIVE CONTEXT TO THE POINT THE AUTHOR IS MAKING THAT "AND" IS THE KEY TO HAPPINESS AND SUCCESS. BY ITALICIZING THE WORD "AND" IN THESE EXAMPLES, AND THROUGHOUT THE ESSAY, THE WRITER HAMMERS HOME THE IDEA THAT THIS WORD IS CENTRAL TO HIS PERSONAL JOURNEY AND STORY.

Is not doubt the exact opposite of the faith to which Christians are called? Yet, maturing in my faith has brought me to doubt. Ignoring my own questions inevitably leads me in the wrong direction. Just as the Theory of Relativity was cemented in our understanding of the universe by constant attempts to disprove it, one can sharpen one's faith with the iron that is doubt. Paradoxically, the combination of faith *and* doubt strengthens us.

Born in Havana, Cuba, my maternal grandmother found asylum in the United States when Castro came to power in 1959, separated from all that she knew and loved. When the experience of losing everything is ingrained in our memory, we are rightfully fearful of repeating the past. Yet, hearing and feeling the priceless story of her previous life bonds me with my grandmother as we share our hopes with each other. Embracing the stories of my grandmother's past helps keep our traditions alive. We must understand the past and why it happened, *and* simultaneously dream and hope. The study of history betters our future. Past *and* future need each other just as my grandmother and I need each other.

On the court, at the dinner table, and in college, symbiotic relationships, rather than individualism, make life better. A prosperous classroom builds off of the discoveries of its students *and* teachers, for the greater good. A successful sports team is one that celebrates and benefits from individual *and* group accomplishments. A [country] obsessed with the other side failing, rather than pushing for the general prosperity of all citizens, is destined for collapse. While competition helps motivate us, winning is not defined by the defeat of another. Shared success, of the individual *and* of the group, strengthens all of us. The combination of individualism *and* pursuit of the greater good is unbeatable.

Living by the "and" is an ongoing process. I want to study practical things *and* the "just because" things. Some in the business world are not often portrayed as loving and considerate, but I cannot compromise on this. Business *and* morality need not be enemies. I want to study economics *and* ethics, statistics *and* Shakespeare.

I choose to think *and* to feel. I choose to laugh *and* to cry. I choose to celebrate now *and* dream of then. I choose to snooze *and* be on time.

Joseph I. Malchow

Scotch Plains-Fanwood High School
Scotch Plains, NJ

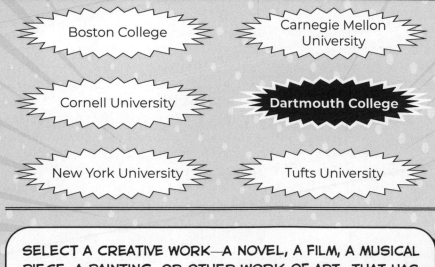

Boston College

Carnegie Mellon University

Cornell University

Dartmouth College

New York University

Tufts University

SELECT A CREATIVE WORK—A NOVEL, A FILM, A MUSICAL PIECE, A PAINTING, OR OTHER WORK OF ART—THAT HAS INFLUENCED THE WAY YOU VIEW THE WORLD AND THE WAY YOU VIEW YOURSELF. DISCUSS THE IMPACT THE WORK HAS HAD ON YOU.

IDEAS

Ah, *Figaro*! I am fortunate to at last have an opportunity to pour the gallons of zest inspired by that name into words that, hereto, have gone unexpressed. Perhaps, when complete, this essay will further serve to retort my parents' incredulous stares when *"La Vendetta!"* blares resolutely, in all its Mozartian glory, from those faithful woofers atop my dresser.

Mozart and Da Ponte's *Le Nozze Di Figaro,* The Marriage of Figaro, has done much for me. It has ushered my musical palette forth with breathtaking speed. But within this single work there also exists a bevy of culture that touches all aspects of human interest! Where else but in the audience of an opera can one be diverted, learn music, language, and history all simultaneously? Can anything else residing on three modest compact discs take a person as many months to digest and fully enjoy? In my eighteen years I've experienced nothing like the thrill of the opera. The profits I have reaped from my experience with *Figaro* have been invaluable. For all of the listening, viewing, and reading that I have done—for all of those hours happily occupied—I am beginning to absorb the Italian language, socioeconomic class-relations of 18th century Europe, and Spanish dress and architecture. In this way, opera, and more specifically *Figaro*—my first—has spilt light upon previously shadowed intellectual interests.

Though I revere *Figaro*'s superlative educational utility, the piece synapses with me on a personal level as well. In its essence, opera seeks to communicate. In Peter Shaffer's play *Amadeus*, Antonio Salieri, describing the raw emotive puissance of Mozart's work, says, "I heard the music of true forgiveness filling the theatre, conferring on all who sat there a perfect absolution." Opera demands the synergy of all of mankind's methods of communication—song, acting, dance, oratory, and music. I was first introduced—truly introduced—to *Figaro* at the Metropolitan Opera in New York City. I invited my closest friends there for my eighteenth birthday. I had already read much of the libretto and heard Sir Georg Solti's *Figaro* on compact disc. But as I sat in the audience—subtitles steadily glowing from the LCD screen before me—I saw the majesty of opera blossom in real time. I saw comedy, tragedy, and villainy at once; invoking so many tools—so perfectly—to deliver the milieu of each and every scene. I had always held myself to be a person of communication; English and Literature had always been my favorite class. But I sat there, viewing the work of this man, who I'd always heard limned as 'great', in absolute control of his audience. And I whispered to myself—I recall this vividly—, "I get it." I understood why his bust was placed below the headline "The Great Composers" on that poster in 3rd grade music class. As I viewed John Relyea's Figaro bouncing to the pulse of *Non Piu Andrai* under James Levine's stewardship, I knew that this was an art form I could appreciate.

THE AUTHOR INVITES US INTO THEIR THOUGHTS BY DETAILING A PROFOUND "AH-HA!" MOMENT. ADDING PERSONAL DETAILS, EMOTIONS, AND THOUGHTS GETS TO THE CORE OF THE PERSONAL STATEMENT: INVITING THE READER TO GET TO KNOW THE WRITER ON A DEEPER LEVEL THAN WHAT IS ALREADY PROVIDED IN THE APPLICATION.

Julia C.
Mount Saint Dominic Academy
New Jersey

Fordham University

George Washington University

Providence College

DISCUSS AN ACCOMPLISHMENT, EVENT, OR REALIZATION THAT SPARKED A PERIOD OF PERSONAL GROWTH AND A NEW UNDERSTANDING OF YOURSELF OR OTHERS.

IDEAS

"ROCK 'N' CONFIDENCE"

The early morning sky, tinged with hues of orange and pink, frames my distorted reflection in the beveled glass doors. I am a spirited sixteen-year-old in my barista apron, holding up a golden key. I close my eyes, inhale deeply, and whisper, *"you got this."* I insert the key into the keyhole and exhale as I unlock the Rock 'n' Joe Coffee Bar doors for the first time. As the newly promoted manager, I am overwhelmed with gratitude, happiness, and a sense of accomplishment. My boss believes in me; he trusts me. *I feel confident.*

> THIS REFERENCE TO A GOLDEN KEY HOLDS LITERAL AND FIGURATIVE MEANING. THE READER'S IMAGINATION IS PIQUED AND WE ARE INSPIRED TO LEARN MORE ABOUT WHAT THIS KEY UNLOCKS.

The whiff of fresh pastries and loaves of bread stacked neatly along the lower door jamb distracts me. I bend to gather the pastries and loaves of bread, and their warmth comforts me. As I enter, I am greeted by my favorite smells of espresso, powdered sugar, and chocolates. It never gets old. I place the pastries onto the countertop and glance at the cozy nooks and walls filled with rock n roll memorabilia. The shop *looks* the same, but today it *feels* different. I am accountable. I begin my routine of brewing coffees, heating grills, and polishing the glass pastry case. I finish prepping and artfully chalk today's daily special on the old-school chalkboard: The *Lov'n'Latte*. I turn up the volume of coffee shop tunes adding to the positive vibe and morning mood.

I am lost in happy thoughts when Chef Geo enters with his three-year-old daughter, Fía, on his shoulders. They're cheering in Spanish. She sees me. Her cheer erupts into laughter, and we hug good morning. Fía speaks Spanish, but our joyful interactions are fluent. She shows me her newly painted nails of glittery pinks and purples, then squeals in delight as she points to our breakfast of

Cinnamon Cigars. I place her small hand in mine and lead her to our "VIP" table. We "toast" with our cigars and laugh as the cinnamon sugar forms our powdery mustaches. I am so happy Fía is part of my world. I know my first day as a manager is already a good one.

My managerial experience over the past year has given me tremendous insight into how the world works. I have a heightened awareness of how my leadership impacts those who trust me. I have a sense of accountability and responsibility not only to my boss but also to my staff. What I appreciate most, however, are the opportunities to engage with my customers. My friends and family have told me I have a knack for making others feel good about themselves. So, naturally, I love striking up conversations about life, handing out pastries as after-school treats, and inspiring customers to try new coffees or just practicing being a good listener.

Rock 'n' Joe is much more than a "rock 'n' cup of joe." It's where the community comes to connect, and it is my mission to ensure that the atmosphere is always warm and inviting, the energy is positive, and smiles are contagious. Customers come to Rock 'n' Joe and put the weight of the world down, if even just for a moment. Balancing life can feel so intimidating some days that it seems impossible to prioritize, but at Rock 'n' Joe, it's easy. *People are my priority.*

THIS CONCLUSION BRINGS THE ESSAY FULL CIRCLE AND WRAPS IT UP BEAUTIFULLY FOR THE READER. THE WRITER'S DAY IS OVER AND SHE LITERALLY AND FIGURATIVELY CLOSES THE DOOR THAT SHE OPENED IN HER INTRODUCTION.

As I pull the doors closed for the evening, I feel for the key in my loosely slung apron and notice my disheveled reflection. I remind myself that I have served a lot of coffee, but more importantly, I have served a lot of love. As I turn my golden key, I take a moment to reflect. In a world that has fast become upended, I am truly happy and feel balanced. *I am confident.*

June Ankrom

The Pine School
Florida

Ithaca College

Smith College

Wheaton College
(MA)

SHARE AN ESSAY ON ANY TOPIC OF YOUR CHOICE.
IT CAN BE ONE YOU'VE ALREADY WRITTEN, ONE THAT
RESPONDS TO A DIFFERENT PROMPT, OR ONE OF YOUR
OWN DESIGN.

IDEAS

What I like most about museums is the quiet. There's something about walking into a room in a museum (preferably one that is empty and dimly-lit), and sitting to observe. With a cold bench beneath me, no-one else around, maybe the distant echo of footsteps - that for me is where I find solitude. Whether it be the observation of art, or my own thoughts, I find museums to be the most peaceful places for contemplation.

The Gibbes Museum of Art in Charleston, South Carolina has always been among my favorites. On a recent visit, I found a new view from a bench looking into a large, arched doorway, and into this open, bright, naturally-lit room with its glass-domed ceiling and marble busts tucked in each corner. An old man across the way stared at the same tiled floor as I did. Instead of sketching art like I normally would, I sat and sketched this man and the doorway; this new perspective the museum had granted me was art within itself. I had seen the works surrounding me before, but I hadn't seen this man or this specific scene. A new experience with each museum visit is something I cherish. Moments are shared between strangers, without the need to speak.

THE WRITER SETS THE SCENE WITH A VIVID DESCRIPTION OF HER VIEW. THIS USE OF DESCRIPTION BRINGS THE READER INTO THE ESSAY AND KEEPS THEM ENGAGED.

A personal belief of mine is that you shouldn't be allowed to talk in museums. This is not to suggest that I don't have lots to say about the art I view. But I feel it is more valuable to save those thoughts for a conversation once you've left. First, have a conversation with yourself and the art, and then speak about it with others. I am actually quite a talkative person in most settings, but It seems that once I've entered a museum, I go quiet. My insides light up and all of my senses heighten, but my vocal chords rest.

I think the silence within a museum only adds to the beauty of the artwork. Outside the walls of a museum, my thoughts tend to be louder and to jump from notion to concept to opinion. Inside, my mind is quiet. Even my footsteps are muted, and I feel like I am floating, as if on a cloud. Even if I don't know my way around a museum, I never feel lost. As an artist, I am drawn to create more naturalistic pieces, but in the museum I am not limited to works that resemble my own craft. There's a favorite photo of me, at age six, taken by my father, in which I face a Jackson Pollock. I couldn't have known what I was looking at, but I am still, hands clasped behind my back, dwarfed by the magnitude of the painting. I am alone, but unbothered by this. I am unfazed by the painting. Maybe this love of museums was genetic. My parents are art people.

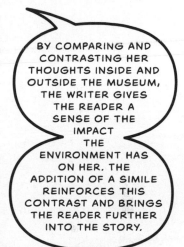

BY COMPARING AND CONTRASTING HER THOUGHTS INSIDE AND OUTSIDE THE MUSEUM, THE WRITER GIVES THE READER A SENSE OF THE IMPACT THE ENVIRONMENT HAS ON HER. THE ADDITION OF A SIMILE REINFORCES THIS CONTRAST AND BRINGS THE READER FURTHER INTO THE STORY.

My six-year old self isn't such a departure from today, but I bring more practical experience to the contemplation of art. I imagine an artist's evolution to create a piece, especially one as abstract as a Pollock. And yet, despite the questions I may have as a viewer, understanding a piece is secondary to the meditative practice of sitting in silence, taking in my environment completely. All my senses are engaged. For me, a peace beyond words can be found while looking into the eyes of a portrait of a woman I haven't and will never know.

I don't attend church, though I know people find solitude and inspiration inside a temple or religious space. Maybe my parish is within the walls of a museum. Though I haven't felt welcomed within the walls of a chapel, my congregation always leads back to works of art.

Karen A. Lee
Garland High School
Texas

Duke University

John Hopkins University

Rice University

Southern Methodist University

Stanford University

HOW HAS THE PLACE IN WHICH YOU LIVE INFLUENCED THE PERSON YOU ARE? DEFINE "PLACE" ANY WAY THAT YOU LIKE . . . AS A CONTEXT, A COUNTRY, A CITY, A COMMUNITY, A HOUSE, A POINT IN TIME.

IDEAS

THE LAND DOWN HERE

When it rains, the inhabitants where I live are the last to know. Welcome to Short People Land. At an early height of four feet eleven inches, I thought I had solidly established residence in the People of Average Height Land. Nonetheless, as I noticed myself moving toward the front of class pictures over the years and I remained four feet eleven inches on my twelfth birthday, I obtained Short Person status. While my personality has its roots in my childhood Average Height Land, becoming and remaining short has greatly influenced the person I am now.

A HOOK CAN BE SHORT (NO PUN INTENDED) AND SWEET, OR SPAN THE ENTIRE INTRODUCTORY PARAGRAPH. THE AUTHOR HAS DONE AN EXCELLENT JOB AT HOOKING THE READER IMMEDIATELY WITH THESE FIRST TWO SENTENCES.

Because I have not reached adulthood, human thought can naturally mistake me for someone younger. For instance, due to the limited size of our school's gymnasium, ninth-grade students are barred from pep rallies. When I tried to attend my first one as a sophomore, students behind me shouted, "Freshman! Go back to class!" I never forget that this confusion will not end with graduation. Employers and coworkers may view me as immature and inexperienced based solely on my height. Keeping this possibility in mind, I consistently put forth extra effort to exceed expectations until perfectionism became automatic. My physics teacher handed back my second lab report of the year with a comment that my lab reports bordered on overkill. I hoped to transform my height into an asset, a trait to make me and my meticulous care stand out in others' memories. My work is by no means flawless, but living in Short People Land encourages my industrious attempts to prove that height and ability are not directly related.

On the other hand, being petite has always brought me the warmth of human companionship. As a short child, I had advantages in certain games, and my playmates welcomed the challenge of playing against me. In hide-and-seek, I would be the only one to fit under a table in the back of a closet under a staircase. I was one of the last people left in limbo. Many of these early diversions gave birth to long-standing friendships. When the stress mounts, we still rely on each other for commiseration. On another occasion, my Short Person citizenship helped me bridge the freshman-senior gap. When the seniors in the International Baccalaureate program at my school formed a club to tutor underclassmen, those who arrived for tutoring were too intimidated to ask for help. I joined a group of ninth-grade girls and casually discussed their biology lab with them. Until ten minutes into the discussion, they had thought I was just another freshman, but by that time, we had overcome their fear, and they gladly accepted me as their official biology tutor. I cannot describe my gratification when one of my protégées stopped me excitedly in the hall, "I made a B on my biology test! Thank you so much!"

While I accept my height with open arms, I recognize all the small annoyances packaged with it. For several years before I turned sixteen, I feared not being able to drive. I had difficulty seeing over the steering wheel and reaching the accelerator with my foot at the same time. In large tour groups at the art museum, I end up memorizing the back of patrons' shirts rather than enjoying the masterpieces. Window blinds are adjusted so that glaring sunlight just misses everyone's eyes but mine. Remembering my own frustrations, I developed a sympathy for others' aggravations and a sensitivity to others' needs. I can empathize with lefties trying to use a right-handed mouse or pale people who sunburn easily, both of whom, like me, suffer simply because of a physical characteristic. I remember to adjust the music stand in orchestra so that my stand partner can also read the music. At a pre-college summer program at Southern Methodist University, my apparent intuition for helping others earned me the nickname "Mother." People came to me for first aid, pocket change, or advice. Probably my limited caretaking talents did not quite deserve my honorable nickname, but I always did my best to help and always felt

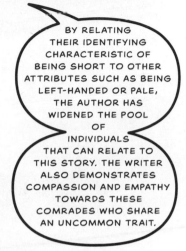

BY RELATING THEIR IDENTIFYING CHARACTERISTIC OF BEING SHORT TO OTHER ATTRIBUTES SUCH AS BEING LEFT-HANDED OR PALE, THE AUTHOR HAS WIDENED THE POOL OF INDIVIDUALS THAT CAN RELATE TO THIS STORY. THE WRITER ALSO DEMONSTRATES COMPASSION AND EMPATHY TOWARDS THESE COMRADES WHO SHARE AN UNCOMMON TRAIT.

content that they appreciated my efforts. Despite their inconveniences, irritations of the vertically challenged mostly disappear before one of Short People Land's finest fruits, a sense of humor. Even I can laugh when someone quips, "You're so short you could pole vault with a toothpick." Knowing I would not take offense, my history teacher used me as an example for situations in which trying as hard as possible may still fail. He asked me to jump and touch the ceiling. I actually came within six inches, but I joined the class in laughing at the ridiculousness of his demand.

My residency in Short People Land has shaped my capacity for diligence, camaraderie, empathy, and laughter. Thanks to my height, I have nearly everything required to attack the ordeals of life and still maintain sanity. Neither have I lost respect for the people up there, so please do not hesitate to bend down. I'll meet you in the Land Down Here.

Katharine Anne Thomas
Lancaster Catholic High School
Pennsylvania

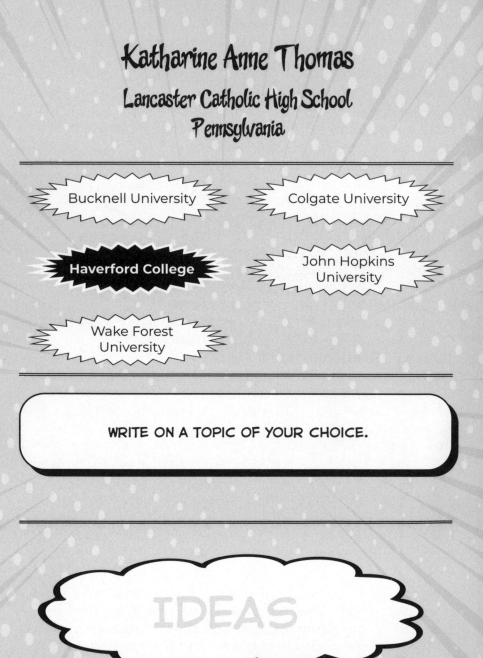

Bucknell University

Colgate University

Haverford College

John Hopkins University

Wake Forest University

WRITE ON A TOPIC OF YOUR CHOICE.

IDEAS

My first real college writing assignment: five neat pages of argument and examples, insightful prose in black type and white space where my professor could write little words of praise. I replayed a little daydream I had developed of him reading the paper, pausing and nodding at the particularly insightful points, scribbling excitedly in the margins and finally closing it with a satisfied sigh. The reason I was looking forward to getting my work back was not that I truly believed it was a work of genius. My sleep-deprived, bleary-eyed misery refused to let me be a fan of my work. At that point I was cursing the uncountable nights of rubbing my temples in the unforgiving glow of the computer screen I had spent on it. Instead, my prediction was based on precedent (not to mention each aching bone's demand for restitution). Teacher's responses to my work had always been positive, and I grew increasingly confident about my ability. But in the process, my purpose in writing shifted from self expression as it should be in its purest form and instead to gaining recognition.

Upon reading the paper, my professor suggested that I take a second look at it. His comments clarified ideas that had always been beyond my grasp. So many of my papers with similarly obscured errors had gone without being criticized, but, strangely enough, no red-inked "Fantastic!" was nearly as gratifying as having my own vague sense of flaw verified. While other teachers' compliments had been flattering, what I appreciated more than anything, and what I would require to become any better in my craft, was a healthy dose of criticism. I realized that being selective enough in choosing my words would ensure that my ideas would never be misunderstood.

WHILE COLLEGE ESSAYS SHOULD HIGHLIGHT POSITIVE ATTRIBUTES OF THE APPLICANT, ADDRESSING HOW OVERCOMING A STRUGGLE OR OBSTACLE CAN MAKE AN EXCELLENT CHOICE OF TOPIC. THE AUTHOR PINPOINTS A SPECIFIC FLAW THAT SERVED AS AN OPPORTUNITY FOR LEARNING.

Envisioning the images that words have the power to create restored my passion for writing. What had made me love writing initially was the gloriously specific nature of words that enables them to provoke the exact response we intended them to and convey the most complex of emotions more so than any other outlet. Had I meant that Catholicism pervaded Irish tradition or was the religion embedded within culture? Did Joyce's Stephen Dedalus stray from the church or lose his faith? If there hadn't been a deadline I could have worked on that paper for weeks, editing day and night and probably still not being fully satisfied. I was at fault for having the haughtiness that led me to believe that I manipulated words, when in fact the opposite is true. Their role as the messenger of thought demands reverence. Words are for me what shapes and colors are for artists, what notes and beats are for musicians. But the medium by which we choose to express ourselves has little bearing; it need only fulfill its purpose. I gained from this experience a realization that I cannot be above laws that govern mankind's communication. The ability of words to touch one's core is timeless and beyond our grasp.

Kathleen B. Blackburn

Lord Botetourt High School
Virginia

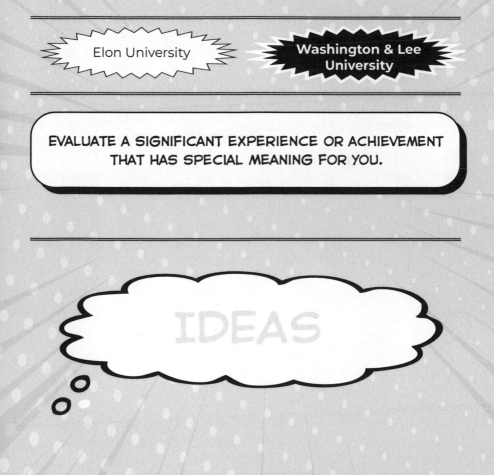

Elon University

Washington & Lee University

EVALUATE A SIGNIFICANT EXPERIENCE OR ACHIEVEMENT THAT HAS SPECIAL MEANING FOR YOU.

IDEAS

It was an odd feeling, riding in the back of that dump truck, a coffin right beside me. As we bounced along the unpaved, potholed, Nicaraguan roads, it would unhinge just a bit, and I could see where Papá would soon be laid. After a long ride under the oppressive sun, the dump truck full of teenagers finally arrived at the tiny home that Mamá and Papá shared, and we unloaded our somber cargo. As I walked up their rocky, dirt yard, I was filled with memories.

> BY SETTING THE PHYSICAL SCENE WITH DESCRIPTIVE LANGUAGE AND IMAGERY, THE WRITER HAS HELPED THE READER VISUALIZE WHERE THE STORY IS TAKING PLACE.

> IN ADDITION, THE AUTHOR SETS THE EMOTIONAL TONE OF THE ESSAY IN THIS INTRODUCTION SO THAT THE READER KNOWS HOW THE WRITER IS FEELING FROM THE VERY BEGINNING.

I had met Mamá and Papá a year earlier, while on my first trip to Nicaragua with Because We Care Ministries. Both were in their eighties and living in filth. Stray dogs would come by their shack and roll in their meager food supply, actually passing mange to Mamá and Papá. The ministry found the poor couple and began to help them, providing food and medicine, teaching them cleanliness habits, such as not to eat food after a dog has urinated on it, and even building them a real home. I remember visiting while their home was under construction. Mamá gave everyone hugs and refused to sit down in the presence of her visitors, despite her dwindling health. Papá was healthy enough to stand and thanked each of us over and over again.

And now, just a year later, we were helping Mamá make the final preparations for Papá's death and burial. While the men lugged the coffin in and placed it in the corner of the one-room home, I rushed to the hammock to see Papá. His blank face stared back at me as he struggled to breathe. The air around him reeked of stale sweat, urine and vomit. I stroked his shriveled hand as his daughter attempted to give him a thimble full of water, but he was too ill to keep it down, and vomited it into a large pan filled with similar substances. At this point, I could not hold it back anymore, and slow tears fell down my face. It just did not seem fair. The only difference between Papá and me was where we happened to be born. Had I been Nicaraguan by birth, I would be in his situation; he would look upon me with pity. Then it was time to gather around Papá for prayer. We all held hands, and I rested my hand upon his bony shoulder. As we began to pray, it seemed as if a fresh breath of life blew into him. He began to pray with us, shouting "¡Gloria a Dios!" with the little strength he could muster. Fresh tears fell from everyone's eyes as the dying man whispered the Spanish words to "Amazing Grace" while we sang in English. Forgetting the strict rules about sanitation and disease, I kissed his sweaty forehead and whispered, "Vaya a casa, Papá. Go home, Papá."

The images of Papá on his deathbed praising the Lord will be forever imprinted in my mind. When I get frustrated with my blessed life in my comfortable Virginia home, I remember the amazing faith of this man. When I am disappointed, I remember the greater disappointments he faced. When I am weak, I remember how much weaker he was. And when I am joyful, I remember his immense joy, which makes me even gladder.

Papá did go home two days after I last saw him. Because of our shared faith, I firmly believe that he is in the presence of God. I cannot imagine how exciting heaven is for him. All he ever knew were the dirt roads of Nicaragua; now he walks along streets of gold. He was always ill; now he is in the presence of the Great Physician. He spent most of his life living in a trash bag; now he inhabits his own mansion. He never had quite enough beans and rice; now he has more than he could ever want. He taught me and so many others so much about life in the short time we knew him; I cannot wait to see him, wrap my arms around his thick, healthy body and say gracias.

Kayla L.
Immaculate Heart Academy
New Jersey

Fordham University   Villanova University

SOME STUDENTS HAVE A BACKGROUND, IDENTITY,
INTEREST, OR TALENT THAT IS SO MEANINGFUL
THEY BELIEVE THEIR APPLICATION WOULD BE
INCOMPLETE WITHOUT IT. IF THIS SOUNDS LIKE YOU,
THEN PLEASE SHARE YOUR STORY.

IDEAS

"UN ESPRIT OUVERT"

At an early age, I realized cultural diversity is not just about one's ethnicity and language, but also the way one lives their life. My mother migrated from the Dominican Republic to the United States at an early age and eventually met my father, who is Peruvian. I was born soon after. My parents both worked long nights and my grandmother "abuela" would care for me. I remember the tastes and smells of her home-cooked Dominican arroz con pollo y habichuelas (chicken, rice, and beans) my favorite! If I close my eyes, I can still hear the upbeat Merengue playing in the background. At night, she would softly sing me to sleep with Spanish lullabies. My parents would wake me in the morning, speaking mostly in English.

Growing up in a Hispanic home, I was bilingual, and languages came naturally. My family would celebrate Spanish and Peruvian holidays and customs, often mixing them with pieces of American traditions as we became more immersed in her culture. I loved speaking between Spanish and English and in middle school, I became intrigued by studying another language and chose French. For my graduation, my parents surprised me with a summer trip to Aix-en-Provence, France where I visited my aunt and uncle, whom I had never met.

I arrived at Aix-en-Provence, it was so charming and quaint. I immediately set off to explore. I strolled through the town, visited churches, and shops, and strolled the local marketplace. Toward the end of the day, I slowed down and sat in the middle of the cobblestone square. I wanted to take it all in. As I gazed into the early evening, I noticed a family dining al fresco, friends dancing in the street to the sweet jazz of a passionate saxophone player, and small crowds of young and elderly lingering. It was as if everyone had lost track of time and had nowhere more important to be. It was simple and yet the energy was palpable.

The next morning, I woke excitedly. My aunt and uncle took me to the lively marketplace. They planned to cook an authentic French dinner, and I was the "sous chef". We shopped for the freshest, farm-grown ingredients. While there, I was introduced to friends. I felt intimidated at first and was nervous that when I spoke, my pronunciation might be off, or I would say something wrong or confusing. Nonetheless, I was committed to putting myself out there. I had to move out of my comfort zone. And so I did. I smiled and tried to listen to the conversations and respond appropriately. My aunt and uncle were so happy and I couldn't help but feel proud. The days passed quickly and I started to feel comfortable. I gained confidence. I had real conversations with my relatives and townspeople. I engaged in some of the local customs and traditions. I even attended a French church service and followed along! It was at that moment I realized I wasn't just listening to French but was *understanding it*; *I was connected. I was multilingual.* It was as if time stood still.

THE WRITER HAS DONE A GREAT JOB AT SUMMARIZING THE KEY LEARNINGS OF THEIR EXPERIENCE IN THEIR CONCLUSION. WHILE PERSONAL STATEMENTS DO NOT NEED TO FOLLOW A SPECIFIC ESSAY FORMAT (UNLESS REQUESTED BY THE SCHOOL), WRAPPING UP THE ESSAY WITH MAIN TAKEAWAYS IS A HELPFUL REMINDER TO YOUR READER OF THE MESSAGE YOU ARE CONVEYING IN YOUR STORY.

I loved visiting Aix-en-Provence that summer. I realized my upbringing, curiosity for language, diligent study, and immersion in France had given me not only a sense of independence but a new perspective. I realized that language was not just about words, but about understanding and connection. Reflecting on my trip, I remembered how I spoke, laughed, danced, sang, cooked, and simply connected with my relatives. I now understand I am part of something greater. I gained a worldview and global mind and want to continue to study languages and cultures in college. I have a deep appreciation for my own ethnicity as it has led me to always keep an open mind, or as the French would say, having *un esprit ouvert.*

Kylee Sigler
Cypress Woods High School
Texas

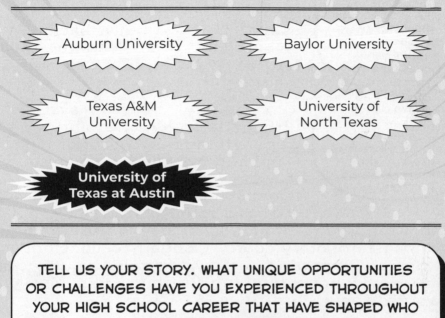

Auburn University

Baylor University

Texas A&M University

University of North Texas

University of Texas at Austin

TELL US YOUR STORY. WHAT UNIQUE OPPORTUNITIES OR CHALLENGES HAVE YOU EXPERIENCED THROUGHOUT YOUR HIGH SCHOOL CAREER THAT HAVE SHAPED WHO YOU ARE TODAY?

IDEAS

Having the wind knocked out of you usually does not lead to an emergency dentist visit, but there I was, staring into the luminescent light. I was shaking, my mouth was numb, and I didn't remember how I got there. I could faintly hear my mom and another person talking. I soon realized that my mom was talking to a doctor about me. "Is my baby okay?" "Can you put it back in?" "What does this mean for the future?" "How long will recovery take?"

BY SETTING THE SCENE FOR THE READER WITH DETAILS AND IMAGERY, THE AUTHOR IS ENCOURAGING THE READER TO VISUALIZE THE STORY AS IT PLAYS OUT IN THE ESSAY. THESE DETAILS HELP DRAW THE READER INTO THE MOMENT AND EXPERIENCE IT FOR THEMSELVES.

In January, I was an average fifth grader, but come February, I was anything but. One afternoon, I grabbed my bike and went out to ride with friends. Less than twenty minutes later, my life changed forever. I was now not an average fifth grader. I was now a fifth grader with a temporary tooth. I began to constantly worry about getting hurt; I was afraid I would get hurt again, not something a fifth grader typically worries about.

My doctors told me that at some point, I would need to get an implant on my front tooth.

That moment came during my junior year. I left for Christmas break with what at least looked like a tooth in and was coming back with an empty smile. While I had a retainer that kind of looked like a tooth, I was worried everyone would be able to see that underneath it, I was toothless. I became increasingly anxious that my peers would figure out my secret.

True to my worst fears, my first day back from Christmas break was a bit of a nightmare. I felt like everyone could see right through my retainer, like they knew I had undergone surgery and didn't have a tooth. I, a normally extroverted person, became self-conscious and distanced myself from friends; I did not tell them about the surgery and did not want them to find out. I devoted entirely too much energy wondering if people could see through my act.

Then, one day, I thought, "so what if people know I don't have a front tooth? If they treat me differently, that's their problem, not mine." I realized that if the people I surrounded myself with were not understanding of my surgery, then I did not want them to be around me. After my realization, my self-confidence grew. This growth was not confined to just my appearance. I became more confident with public speaking and giving presentations. I changed the narrative and became more positive. This newfound confidence and positivity inspired me to take the initiative and start a new club at my school that I had wanted to create. It also led me to get out of my comfort zone and apply for a leadership position in my school's chapter of the National Honor Society. The only thing that had been holding me back from starting my club and applying for a leadership position was a lack of confidence. I was worried about speaking in front of large groups and being in charge, but I am not anymore. I am now President of my club, an executive board member for my school's chapter of NHS, and a representative for my school at my district's Superintendent Student Leadership Advisor Council.

Throughout the next chapter of my life, I will continue getting the wind knocked out of me. But now, I can confidently answer my mother's question; her baby will be okay. The challenges I went through to learn a tooth would give me the confidence of a lifetime is something that I will remember every time I smile. I am excited to see where my increased confidence and positivity will take me. I am ready to tackle the uncertainty of college life and excited for the opportunities to come.

Liam Quan
South Carolina

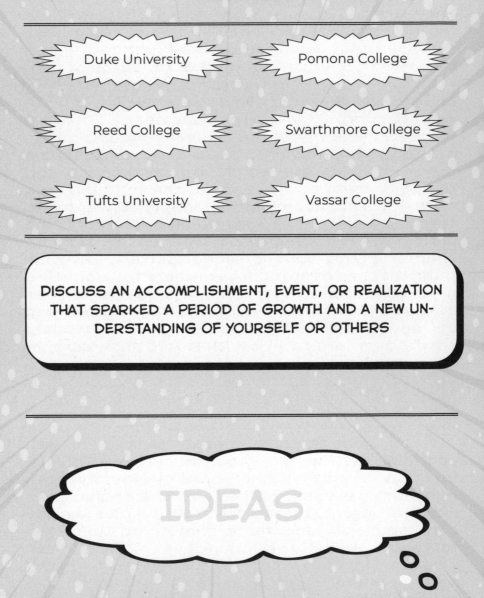

Duke University

Pomona College

Reed College

Swarthmore College

Tufts University

Vassar College

DISCUSS AN ACCOMPLISHMENT, EVENT, OR REALIZATION THAT SPARKED A PERIOD OF GROWTH AND A NEW UNDERSTANDING OF YOURSELF OR OTHERS

IDEAS

I was panicking in a Manhattan Nordstrom that smelled like soggy paper and stale perfume: the carefully collated labels were suffocating. Segregated by size, age, gender, and other ways to split apart an identity, the store reminded me that I couldn't be placed on any single rack.

BY USING A METAPHOR TO FORESHADOW THE THEME OF THE ESSAY, THE WRITER HAS TIED TOGETHER THIS ENGAGING ANECDOTE AND THEIR LARGER MESSAGE, LEAVING THE READER WANTING TO KNOW MORE.

I hyperventilated in a colorless changing room, wanting to run away, but I didn't. My friend Kelsey was waiting for me. I couldn't let him down, so I calmed myself with curiosity. Dresses in the corner—I'd never worn one. How would it feel? Like opening the freezer after sweating in a heat wave. Startling, soothing…and smelling like a department store. However, I made the mistake of looking at the sign for the fitting room: "Men." I paused. Contemplated the label. I'm half Jewish and half Vietnamese, birthed from fish sauce and rugelach. I like boys and am attracted to girls. Apparently, now I wear dresses. Did all that belong in the men's changing room? The Deep South's hospitality doesn't extend to everyone—was my gowned reflection safe to bring home?

I'm accustomed to navigating my problems through words; the more I label, the more direction and control I have. But suddenly, in a random Nordstrom, I was battling something that I couldn't contain with consonants: me. I fell back on my usual strategy of laying out what I knew like an unsolved series of crimes, trying to regain composure, but I realized no red string—no label—could connect my identities. So like any prospective writer, scientist, or lawyer, I began to research.

After Manhattan, I was obsessed with scanning the internet for words like "non-binary," "biracial," and "biromantic," thinking a certain combination of categorizations would bring order. But despite what BuzzFeed quizzes said, I didn't feel like a boy, and "girl" didn't fit either—not to mention the other identity crises. Meanwhile, prom (the ultimate declaration of who you are in high school society) snuck up on me. I wanted to wear a dress, yet putting on a tux sounded easier; it would keep me safe physically in South Carolina and label me as something familiar: "boy." But I remembered the brief comfort in the changing room—I remembered what it was like to actually be myself. Ultimately, I felt it in my marrow that I needed to be authentic, and that trumped the potential dangers.

THIS DETAILED DESCRIPTION BRINGS THE READER ALONGSIDE THE WRITER IN THIS MOMENT; THE READER CAN FEEL THE AUTHOR'S ANXIETY AND HEIGHTENED SENSE OF AWARENESS. THIS TYPE OF DESCRIPTIVE WRITING ALLOWS THE READER TO CONNECT WITH THE AUTHOR.

As I strutted to prom in an elegant, obsidian gown, a car slowed down beside me. I'd heard about drive-bys on the news—suddenly, I noticed how immobile heels made me. The mechanical droning of windows rolling grated my ears. Someone stuck their head out. I froze.

"Get it, queen!"

The three women in the car cheered and honked their horn, celebrating me; my classmates followed suit. By the end of prom I'd forgotten that my dress could be dangerous.

That night, a teacher asked,

"Are you still a boy?"

Again, I was struck with the overwhelming urge to spit out a label. Girl. Boy. Something we both could understand. But instead of forcing myself into a white picket paradigm, I leaned into ambiguity:

"I'm not sure."

Surprisingly, it felt true.

I wear dresses and earrings. I kiss boys and also find girls pretty. I eat challah and mooncakes. I have no clue what that makes me, but it can't be condensed into a one-word morsel. And as scary as it is for someone who seeks safety in syllables, I finally let go of trying to write myself down. I realized that I can only be me if I set logic behind, forget about belonging on an orderly Nordstrom rack, and embrace the indescribable chaos of everything I am. Who cares if it's confusing?

Lindsay O'Connor Stern

The Brearley School

Amherst College

WRITE AN ORIGINAL, PERSONAL RESPONSE TO ONE OF SEVERAL QUOTATIONS. THE QUOTATION SELECTED:

"THE WORLD AS REVEALED BY SCIENCE IS FAR MORE BEAUTIFUL, AND FAR MORE INTERESTING, THAN WE HAD ANY RIGHT TO EXPECT. SCIENCE IS VALUABLE BECAUSE OF THE VIEW OF THE UNIVERSE THAT IT GIVES."

—GEORGE GREENSTEIN, PROFESSOR OF ASTRONOMY, AMHERST COLLEGE

IDEAS

TOCK, TICK

On the evening my grandmother died, I built a time machine. Unconscious of the link between my shock and my invention, I hauled my parents' stationary bike into my room and taped a calendar to the handlebars. With crayon I crossed out the current date and drew a star in the box before it. I climbed on, closed my eyes and pedaled, thrilled that I'd forgotten a brake.

Nine years older and with a tamer imagination, I remember my device with something more than amusement. It was less a response to loss, I realize, than evidence of my skepticism about time and how we perceive it. Clocks have always made me uneasy, if not for their monotony, then for their mechanical precision. I wondered how days could hinge on such featureless percussion. Most unsettling was the thought that the clicking of little wheels could harness time.

This childhood concern extended far beyond my watch; I rejected confinement in any form. My school planners lay unopened, my Saturdays free. I scrawled assignments in page margins, lost myself in books, and designed my own language. In Middle School I worked best after dark, saving my homework till late so I could race against the clock. When I learned to sail, I spent hours in a tub-sized boat on the Connecticut River, leaning from the rim until I capsized and came up spluttering, delighted at my own nerve.

After years of living literally on the edge, I sat down with my uncle for a lecture on relativity. As he explained the details behind Einstein's famous equation—the logic of temporal dilation—I was first puzzled, then suspicious. Time, it seemed, was more malleable than I'd realized. I slipped outside to test the theory. Stopwatch in hand, I made my way to the corner of the yard. I crouched, then dashed across the lawn, staring hard at the digital display. Would my small machine reflect what my uncle described, that each second was entirely subjective? If Einstein were right, which I suspected he was, shouldn't speed slow time, however slightly? If it did, the blinking numbers betrayed nothing.

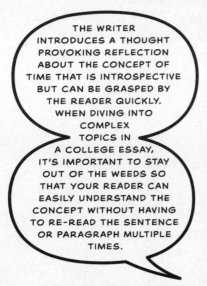

THE WRITER INTRODUCES A THOUGHT PROVOKING REFLECTION ABOUT THE CONCEPT OF TIME THAT IS INTROSPECTIVE BUT CAN BE GRASPED BY THE READER QUICKLY. WHEN DIVING INTO COMPLEX TOPICS IN A COLLEGE ESSAY, IT'S IMPORTANT TO STAY OUT OF THE WEEDS SO THAT YOUR READER CAN EASILY UNDERSTAND THE CONCEPT WITHOUT HAVING TO RE-READ THE SENTENCE OR PARAGRAPH MULTIPLE TIMES.

Relativity, of course, was well beyond my grasp. My experiment was more creative than controlled. And yet, despite my childishness, I learned something else that night: that time was more elaborate than four digits could express. Clocks portrayed the mysterious as the banal, and confined our ultimate abstraction to ticking, two-dimensional space. Their function, I understood, was not to dictate time but to narrate its progression. To my surprise, this realization was liberating; standing breathless on the grass, I felt strangely free.

After several more years, I abandoned rebellion. The more I learned, the more my restlessness subsided. I began to see the world less in terms of its restrictions; through science, I discovered more than I had ever imagined. From magnets to sound waves, from lightening to electrons, life was full of complexities. Each was humbling, but also reassuring; for the first time, I felt that my imagination was validated rather than disproved. While my respect for the world grew profoundly, I continued to dodge convention, and did my best to avoid routine. Perhaps from stubbornness or evasion, or simply because it makes my wrist itch, I still don't wear a watch.

THE AUTHOR'S CONCLUSION WRAPS UP THE ESSAY AND TIES NICELY BACK TO THE THEME OF TIME WITH MENTION OF THE WATCH.

Luke Sommer
St. Louis Priory School
Missouri

Chicago State University

Drexel University

Fordham University

Lawrence University

Loyola University Chicago

Miami University

St. John's University

Truman State University

University of Dayton

SHARE AN ESSAY TOPIC OF YOUR CHOICE.

IDEAS

BROKEN LESSONS

"But I endure, if you know what I mean."

—Richard Farina, *Been Down So Long It Looks Like Up to Me*

Icebreakers often commence workshops and group events. A frequently encountered icebreaker requires members of the group to state their name and an interesting fact about themselves. My response: my name is Luke, and I've broken twenty-three bones.

APPROPRIATE USE OF HUMOR IN A COLLEGE ESSAY IS APPRECIATED. ADMISSIONS READERS REVIEW SCORES OF APPLICATIONS, AND A GOOD CHUCKLE MAKES A MEMORABLE ESSAY.

Kindergarten saw a bright red kickball sweep my stubby legs from under me, leaving my forehead cracked upon impact. I was rushed to the hospital where I received seven stitches in my head and a lesson: be more careful. I did not heed this wisdom. One week later I was back in the hospital after a tragic concert-gone-wrong in the shower; I received seven more stitches and several scoldings. The tragedy inspired my first art piece, *Shower Slip:* a piece that won gallery recognition.

Fourth grade ended and I—now a big middle schooler—embraced the freeing release of summer with open arms and ambitions of adventure. I desired to spend my days seizing back stolen time that school had stripped. My plans of treehouses and wheelies were cut short by the worst leg break my orthopedic surgeon had ever witnessed. Boredom drove me to occupy bed-ridden days with anything that made the clock tick faster; I quickly found myself increasingly infatuated with art. Books on modern art inspired a love of Basquiat, Haring, and Warhol; their works unleashed my creativity.

In eighth grade, internal religious conflict, coupled with consistent quarreling with my parents clouded my mind during exam week, with nagging foot pain occasionally piercing my concentration; I had broken five bones in my foot. The pain continued to worsen as panic ensued; my physical and mental wellbeing deteriorated into shambles. I found reprise through literature. *Of Mice and Men* cemented my understanding of my life dreams, allowing for the pursuit of happiness and individual goals while simultaneously recognizing injustice and suffering. *Holes* taught me to doubt established norms and look for truths beyond face value. Literature directly transformed my understanding of reality.

I continued to rack up my tally of injuries, as a torn labrum and fractured hip marred my Junior year. The surgery and months spent on crutches became a catalyst for problems at home when tensions between my father and I escalated. Almost every interaction between us resulted in fighting, leading me into a downward spiral, and extensive meetings with child services marked my collision with the spiral's base and a harrowing lesson learned: I am broken.

The one consistency between my breaks, bruises, and tears is one that I am immensely grateful for: I always heal. I lacked a doctor to instruct my mental healing process, but found a surrogate in literature and a committed return to art. Reading and creative release provide lessons, poised questions, expression, and identity; I was humbled and forced to realize that I will spend my entire life learning. Richard Farina's *Been Down so Long it Looks Like Up to Me*

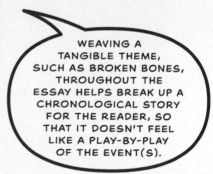

WEAVING A TANGIBLE THEME, SUCH AS BROKEN BONES, THROUGHOUT THE ESSAY HELPS BREAK UP A CHRONOLOGICAL STORY FOR THE READER, SO THAT IT DOESN'T FEEL LIKE A PLAY-BY-PLAY OF THE EVENT(S).

provided respite at my lowest point---demonstrating value in human life especially when in a detestable, grotesque state. Duchamp's *Fountain* and Goya's *Third of May* became windows into a new world; a world where established principles and pressures can be broken: successfully. Avant Garde artists renewed my self-perspective, allowing for me to truly embrace myself, express my individuality through discussion of literature and the creation of poems and stories, put a stained glass window inside of a TV, and began to express myself through fashion after being inspired by *America: A Lexicon in Fashion*, an exhibition at the Metropolitan Museum of Art. I learned a quintessential life lesson: to be myself, no matter the cost.

Maria Inez Velazquez

Springfield High School of Science and Technology
Springfield, MA

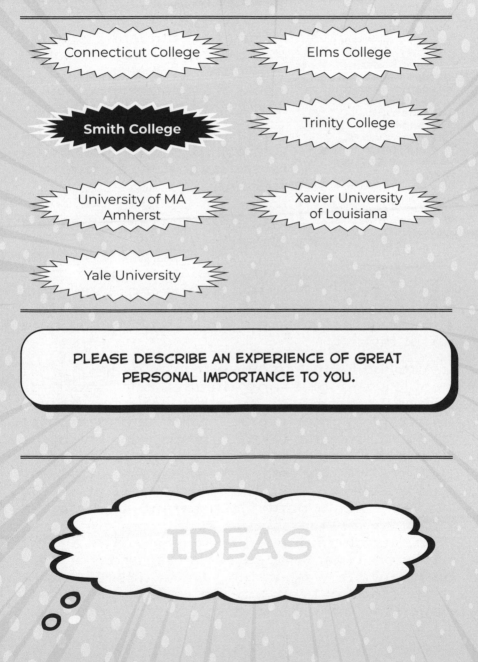

Connecticut College

Elms College

Smith College

Trinity College

University of MA Amherst

Xavier University of Louisiana

Yale University

PLEASE DESCRIBE AN EXPERIENCE OF GREAT PERSONAL IMPORTANCE TO YOU.

IDEAS

IN SEARCH OF SOLITUDE

It is hard to come home again. I'm finding that out now. Over the summer I was stripped away, like an onion, a gradual pruning of all but the essentials. I became purified. I spent the summer as far away from home as I could get: two weeks in New Mexico as a Student Challenge Award Recipient, contemplating unknown constellations; four weeks as a scholarship student at Xavier University in New Orleans.

"I" STATEMENTS CAN BE AN IMPACTFUL WAY TO FOCUS THE PERSONAL STATEMENT AROUND THE WRITER AND DO NOT NEED TO BE AVOIDED. BY CONSISTENTLY USING SHORT "I" STATEMENTS THROUGHOUT THE ESSAY, THE AUTHOR SHOWS THEIR GROWTH THROUGH SYNTAX THAT REPEATS ITSELF. THIS MAKES THE ESSAY PLEASING TO READ WHILE ALSO TELLING A MEANINGFUL PERSONAL STORY.

Leaving home was the scariest part. I have made myself malleable; I am the good student, the understanding friend, the dutiful daughter. I have always defined myself in terms of others: the ways they understood me was the way I was. It is so easy to do that. It is an easing of the mind, a process of surrender, a fading to oblivion, a surrender that kept me from thinking too hard about my self.

After building myself up from a heap of other people's thoughts and dreams, how shocking, then, to emerge into the stark fluorescent lights of an airport, to enter its crass brilliance, and discover I had no self, no one to define me. My plane ride to this new and foreign land of Albuquerque, New Mexico was my first solitary journey, my first layover, my first disembarking; I got off the plane in a cold panic, lost. I frantically tried to disappear once again, to hide from the harsh light. Huddled between the shelves of an airport bookstore I examined myself and found that I was empty. There was nothing there to see. Finally, the passage of time and the glare of the cashier ripped me from the grip of Nullity. Prompted by her look, I grabbed the cheapest, nearest book I could find. The book's weight in my hand was vaguely comforting.

In New Mexico, my book and I are left alone again. I spend the hot, noon bright days letting the glory of bone-white sidewalks burn away my pretensions towards identity. I play lightly with my voice, letting it flit and gravel-throat its way through stories and normal conversation. I experiment with the movement of my body, the inclination of my look. I discover I can be profound. I become outrageous, controversial, glinting glitter-bright fingernails every which way.

Two weeks later, my book and I leave New Mexico. I have memorized its cover: *The Hanged Man* by Francesca Lia Block. We travel onwards to New Orleans; its weight in my hands is again an anchor to reality.

In New Orleans, I am seduced by sepia, absorbed into a heaving mass of hued skin; I gladly lose myself in the balm of sweetly scented hair and cocoa butter. Here, again, I play with my identity. I leave my hair unrelaxed and wear it out. I learn to flash my eyes out, a coquette, and link arms with two girls I have befriended, we three ignoring the catcalls and hoots that track us down the street.

In New Mexico, I discovered the desert night. I let its silence fill me and transform me, until I was at once ethereal, eternal, serene. In New Orleans, I learn to be strong: I am the one the dorm girls come to at night when the black sky has descended and someone has ordered pick-up chicken; I am the one known for being unafraid. By now, I have let my nails grow out, long and blunt, colored them a crimson red – looking at them, I feel taloned and fierce, teeth blackened and filed to a point, like some old Mayan war story. I let my walk mime assertive strides.

It is hard to come home again, to once again surrender to the community of family, friends, and peers, whose chafing needs and desires chafe and brush against the skin with a subtle, bitter susurrus. It is hard to return to school, to the daily routine: I feel sometimes as though the person who claimed mountains is no longer there. But I try to remember this: the human soul is like a deck of tarot cards, and the mind is the dealer. Each card flipped is a facet of the potential self, each card a piece of a new person to be.

"Some of the faces will be mine. I will be the Hanged Man, the Queen of Cups. I will be Strength with her lions."

—*The Hanged Man*, by Francesca Lia Block

Marissa P.

The Academy for Biotechnology at Mountain Lakes
New Jersey

American University

Binghamton University

Brandeis University

Fordham University

Georgetown University

John Jay College of Criminal Justice

New York University

St. John's University

The University of Pennsylvania

SHARE AN ESSAY ON ANY TOPIC OF YOUR CHOICE.

IDEAS

SOMETHING AS SIMPLE AS A STICKER CAN INSPIRE AN ESSAY. IN THIS ESSAY, THE STICKER HOLDS DEEP MEANING. THE WRITER USED A MUNDANE ITEM AND BROUGHT IT TO LIFE WITH HER STORY.

The "NYU DAD" decal sat on the bedside, holding its breath.

Entrusted with the responsibility of raising my half-brother, I accepted the blame for the toddler's scraped knee. As I tended to him, not a single drop of blood dribbled from the wound, yet my father's face bled with red-hot fury. Terrified by his sickening response, I reached for my mother's help. I watched the scene unfold when she arrived: a text considered to be her indifference to the situation unraveled into an intense fight. My cries failed to calm the battle, which soon concluded as my father threatened to leave my mother homeless and steal custody of my sister and me. Wracked with indecision, I deliberated whether I would keep my father in my life after the culmination of his many violations. His nonexistent regret affirmed the decision I still maintain: he will no longer exist in my life merely to harm my family.

Before our relationship's conclusion, my father wavered in and out of his role, even with it clearly spelled out by the purple lettering, D-A-D. Nine years ago, he left us, designing a new family in a separate home, yet I continued fantasizing he was part of mine. His outrage destroyed my illusion, showing that my family consisted solely of three: my mother, sister, and myself.

While we grappled with this new definition of family, I attempted to become a new pillar of stability to ease the vulnerability inflicted by his void. When my older sister cried over middle school math, I sought to assist her. I loathed watching her struggle, so I concerned myself with protecting her, acting as a source of strength for my family. When schoolwork became increasingly challenging for her, I helped teach lessons and checked her assignments. I may be her younger sister, but I strived to support her as a father should.

Assisting my mother proved more difficult as she carried the immeasurable weight of raising a family. When I became more aware of her situation, I tried to share that load how I assumed a D-A-D would. I carried our laundry up the three flights of stairs and assembled things as needed, but eventually, I began contributing financially. I took on every babysitting job possible and worked over 20 hours weekly at the ice cream shop to cover costs, as I still do.

Beyond providing tangible aid, I also support her emotionally. In the process, I learned to balance multiple obligations and matured from these endeavors, yet I began to fear that the role cost me a part of my childhood.

Regardless of these hardships, I always tried to extend my compassion. My fear turned to resentment at how my father's absence necessitated my obligation, and I convinced myself my role demanded the stone-cast image of strength. However, when my father gave me a Christmas present the year I cut him out, the situation forcibly tore down my disguise, leaving me overwhelmed with guilt and desperate for consolation. After years of portraying a resilient figure, my moment of vulnerability led my family to clarify their unwavering support for me.

Their newfound understanding of my emotions eased my situation. My family's unrelenting love helped me redefine my condition no longer as a liability but as a display of love and effort. To reaffirm their empathy, my family gifted me that "NYU Dad" decal after my sister's acceptance to the university. This gift, simply a tiny plastic sticker, cemented my acceptance. Without my father, I evolved to earn the title he rejected. This role of fatherhood, something I once considered a burden, became a symbol. My father's absence, while painful, strengthened my ability to love and care for others, something I'll always continue to do. Now, I proudly hang up my decal, an emblem of my growth forged from these experiences and a reminder of what I still aspire to deserve.

IN THIS SENTENCE, THE WRITER REFERENCES THE STICKER THAT SHE OPENS HER ESSAY WITH AND EXPLAINS ITS MEANING.

THIS REFERENCE GIVES THE READER INSIGHT INTO THE IMPORTANCE OF THAT STICKER AND ADDS CONTINUITY TO THE STORY.

Melissa Henley

McMinnville High School
McMinnville, OR

Dartmouth College

Lewis & Clark College

Linfield College

USE THIS SPACE TO TELL US ANYTHING ELSE ABOUT YOU THAT YOU FEEL WE SHOULD KNOW.

IDEAS

Although it may be difficult to tell, I hate talking about myself. I feel arrogant and self-centered and boastful when I go on and on about what I've done and what I want to do. And since I've had to answer the question "Tell us about yourself" on every other application, whether it's for a college or a scholarship, I've decided not to tell you about myself, but to tell you about my apple tree.

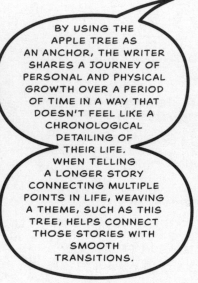

BY USING THE APPLE TREE AS AN ANCHOR, THE WRITER SHARES A JOURNEY OF PERSONAL AND PHYSICAL GROWTH OVER A PERIOD OF TIME IN A WAY THAT DOESN'T FEEL LIKE A CHRONOLOGICAL DETAILING OF THEIR LIFE. WHEN TELLING A LONGER STORY CONNECTING MULTIPLE POINTS IN LIFE, WEAVING A THEME, SUCH AS THIS TREE, HELPS CONNECT THOSE STORIES WITH SMOOTH TRANSITIONS.

I grew up in the country, in a neighborhood where there were only three girls my age, but about ten boys two or more years older than I, one of whom was my obnoxious older brother. With this excess of torture, torment, and testosterone, I was often forced to find places where I could escape the plague of cootie-infested boys. Unfortunately, being both younger and a "girl", I could find no place the boys couldn't go. And so my mother, being the wonderful and patient woman she was, granted me sole access to our apple tree.

Before I continue, I feel I should describe my apple tree to provide you with a mental image as you read on. It's a young tree, no older than I am and so it's rather small, just a bit shorter than our old one-story house. It looks its best in the summer, as most trees do, when it's laden with the greenest and sourest apples imaginable and it's covered with little white blossoms. With all the apples weighing them down, its branches would scratch the ground and form a curtain between the outside world and itself.

My apple tree first gave me respite from the harassment even before I was big enough to actually climb it. I spent days sitting at the base of the tree, writing the oh-so-juicy diary entries of a 7-year old and reading my Serendipity books, separated from the world by a few inches of shrubbery.

After I grew a bit and was able to climb the tree, I spent even more time in it, adding gymnastics and acrobatics (you gain a very unique perspective of the world when you hang by your knees in a tree) to the more peaceful activities of writing and reading. During the school year, when the weather was warm, I would do my homework sitting in my tree and enjoying a snack.

Once I reached middle school, I spent almost as much time in my tree as I did in my bedroom. My writing now included short stories and haikus, usually about nature and animals, and my reading had grown to books with several chapters and little or no pictures (a sacrifice I was forced to make in the effort to find more challenging books). Homework was done at the base of the tree since it was a bit difficult to drag the textbooks up into the branches.

Now, however, at the end of my high school career, I am no longer able to enjoy the comfort and serenity of my apple tree - unless, of course, I want to be prosecuted for trespassing. When my family and I moved from our home in the country, we left behind many things pertinent to the first thirteen years of my life, but my apple tree is what I miss the most.

My apple tree was more than just a refuge from the unbearable boys of the neighborhood. For years, it was my best friend. It was the best listener, with its trunk leaning companionably against my back and its branches hanging above, and it would never reveal any of my feelings or secrets. It was always there for me, strong and dependable, soothing and peaceful.

Meredith Narrowe

King Kekaulike High School
Hawaii

Brown University

Occidental College

Pomona College

Scripps College

Stanford University

HOW HAS THE PLACE IN WHICH YOU LIVE INFLUENCED THE PERSON YOU ARE? DEFINE "PLACE" ANY WAY THAT YOU LIKE . . . AS A CONTEXT, A COUNTRY, A CITY, A COMMUNITY, A HOUSE, A POINT IN TIME.

IDEAS

DA KINE DIVERSITY

He sauntered over from the neighboring display at the National History Day competition at the University of Maryland with an air of superiority.

"So," he drawled, "you three won this category last year? Refresh my memory; what was your project's title?" We turned our attention away from our current History Day display and focused on our competitor.

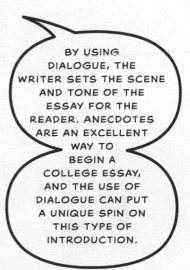

BY USING DIALOGUE, THE WRITER SETS THE SCENE AND TONE OF THE ESSAY FOR THE READER. ANECDOTES ARE AN EXCELLENT WAY TO BEGIN A COLLEGE ESSAY, AND THE USE OF DIALOGUE CAN PUT A UNIQUE SPIN ON THIS TYPE OF INTRODUCTION.

"It was called *Da Kine Talk: Migration to Hawaii Creates Pidgin English . . . And Controversy*," I replied.

"That's right," he conveniently remembered. "What does *da kine* mean, anyway?"

"It's a word you use when you don't know the actual word," I explained. "If you can't remember what color your shoes are, you would say their color is *da kine*."

"It's vague, kind of like 'stuff' or 'whatever,'" interjected my teammate. "For example, when asked what your day's activities will be, your answer would be, 'I'm gonna go *da kine*."

"It's kinda like 'whatchamacalit'," added my other teammate. "If you are frantically searching for your homework assignment and someone asks, 'What are you looking for?' you could reply, 'I can't find my *da kine*!'"

"Oh, I get it," he sneered. "You won last year without knowing what your title means." Haughtily, he turned away. We looked at each other and raised our eyebrows. Although we had given three different answers, each was correct and symbolic of a language that sprouted from

Hawaii's unique cultural diversity. Designed as a means for the *lunas* (overseers) of the canefields to communicate in general terms with laborers of different ethnicities, cultures, and languages, Hawaii's Pidgin English often fails to yield the clear definition our fellow competitor expected.

Hawaii is known as the ethnic and cultural melting pot of the Pacific. It is a place where my parents are Mainland "immigrants," and, I suppose, a place where as a *haole* (Caucasian), I am a minority in my public high school. After growing up in Hawaii, I can discern a thick line between our "island style" and Mainland "normalcy." Like a *keiki* (child) of split custody, I experience both worlds regularly. Sure, I have no clue how to operate a rice cooker, but I do know the difference between Island sticky rice and Uncle Ben's. A good luck cat figurine is absent from my home, but my family follows the custom of removing our rubber slippers before stepping onto our linoleum floor. When I speak with my local friends, I end statements with, "Yeah?" —the customary request for affirmation that your opinion is valid. While attending a three week summer writing program at Carleton College in Minnesota, however, I was surprised to learn that this habit was noticeable and thought of as a Hawaiian "accent" by Mainland students.

Few of my Maui friends would have elected to spend a month of their summer in Minnesota doing *more* schoolwork. In fact, even fewer of my schoolmates, when confronted with the lure of palm-tree lined beaches, would have opted to spend seven months of sunny Sunday mornings enclosed in a house analyzing the effects of Pidgin English on a century of Hawaiian history as my two teammates and I did. By taking advantage of our unique, isolated culture and the abundant amount of information available, we discovered that history is not old and stale, but is a living, personal part of every society. The possibility of supplementing this discovery in a place where everybody has a similar intellectual curiosity and where a never-ending pool of information exists is mind-boggling and exciting. Imagine a child—whose only video viewing experience has been a black and white silent movie—suddenly allowed an unlimited selection of cartoons at the local video store. Stanford is my ultimate video store, an institution in which my beliefs and ideas will be challenged and augmented by more developed views from different backgrounds and perspectives, both inside and outside the classroom. I will find a new *ohana* (family) of people who, like myself, crave new experiences and diverse intellectual pursuits. Again, there will be a variety of answers to any question, all describing *da kine* (truth).

Michael Harris
Plymouth-Whitemarsh High School
Pennsylvania

Boston University

Brandeis University

Duke University

Emory University

George Washington University

Lehigh University

New York University

Tufts University

Washington University in St. Louis

DESCRIBE THE ENVIRONMENT IN WHICH YOU GREW UP AND HOW IT HAS SHAPED YOUR PERSONAL GOALS.

IDEAS

So here I am: another Saturday night, one where I should be out with my friends, enjoying myself, but I am home. I am not here because I am grounded, or because I want to be: instead, I am here to make sure I write the best essay I can and, consequently, be admitted to Tufts University. I realize I only have myself to blame: I have allowed my desire to achieve overtake my longing to be a "normal" high school student.

Upon reaching high school, many students enter the "rebellious teenage years—" the years that disobeying parents is "cool" and having the mentality that less than the best is acceptable. However, I have maintained my drive to achieve despite the temptations to be bitten by the "teenage bug."

Although my friends wonder how, I know exactly why I am just as motivated now as I was ten years ago. Everyone in my family has been extremely successful: they attended top universities and have succeeded in the professional world. Needless to say, from a young age, there was always pressure for me to do just as well. Nothing less than an "A" would suffice, and not a single tangible reward came from my academic achievements.

That personal drive continues to "haunt" me now. Although my family no longer applies nearly as much pressure, I still have that drive to succeed. I accept nothing less than my best, and when I do not achieve up to my capability, I know I have only myself to blame. While the benefits of having a strong work ethic are obvious, I am often jealous of other students who have the luxury of an "average" teenage life.

I often wonder if I should not have allowed my family environment to have that great an impact, and, in turn, let myself learn how to tolerate failure. I no longer have just a desire to succeed: I often feel that I have no choice but to succeed. My stress level often goes off the charts as my goals to achieve and be at my best sometimes make me mentally exhausted.

THE KEY TO A GREAT PERSONAL STATEMENT IS OPENING UP TO THE READER. BY DETAILING HOW THEY MAY HAVE LET EXTERNAL FAMILIAL PRESSURES HOLD TOO MUCH WEIGHT IN THEIR LIFE, THE WRITER HAS OPENED UP AND BECOME VULNERABLE WITH THE READER.

So, as I sit here on Saturday night, writing this essay, I wonder who really has been bitten by the teenage bug: me, or the rest of my graduating class. Should I have let my environment influence me the way it has? Will my drive to succeed actually make me more prepared for the professional world? And, should I have set my personal goals as high as I have?

I do not yet know the answers to my questions, but I truly believe I can find them in my years as an undergraduate student at Tufts. My environment has manifested itself in me, and has become internalized in my own mind. In writing this essay, I have come to realize that it is a mixed blessing: I am fortunate to have such a strong work ethic and desire to achieve, but have not yet experienced the aspects of failure that may await me in the real world.

SUMMARIZING LESSONS LEARNED IN THE CONCLUSION, ESPECIALLY IN AN ESSAY ADDRESSING A TOPIC LIKE PERFECTIONISM, MAKES IT CLEAR TO THE READER THAN THE WRITER HAS GROWN FROM THEIR EXPERIENCE AND CAN APPLY THOSE LESSONS LEARNED IN COLLEGE.

Michael Yelpo
Mountain Lakes High School
New Jersey

This essay was accepted by seven schools; the student prefers not to name them.

SHARE AN ESSAY ON ANY TOPIC OF YOUR CHOICE.

IDEAS

When my family and I returned from our vacation in Rome, everyone naturally asked about the amazing attractions we saw, from the Spanish Steps to the Coliseum. When I explained that I lost myself in a tiny bookshop on a small side street, I was met with looks of surprise, if not actual shock and disbelief. While my friends wouldn't have batted an eye if it was a soccer store, this was a completely different story. They had no idea I would have been so fascinated by such a thing (actually, neither did I).

BY CONTRASTING FAMILIAR TOURIST DESTINATIONS WITH THIS "TINY" BOOK-SHOP, THE WRITER MAKES CLEAR THAT THIS IS NOT GOING TO BE A STEREOTYPICAL STORY. EVEN A PERFECTLY ORDI-NARY BOOKSHOP CAN BECOME SOMETHING OUT OF THE ORDINARY WITH THE RIGHT BIT OF WRITING.

Yet, there I was in a shop full of books that both me (and the average Italian) would not even be able to read. The Libreria Cesaretti specializes in old books, including many that are 400 years old. And that was what caught my eye. And yes, the irony hasn't been lost on anyone. I was literally blocks away from the Coliseum that is over 2000 years old, yet it was the dusty bookshop with wall-to-wall books that captivated me for hours.

When I first walked in, the old many who owned the place appeared to know exactly where every book was located. He was helping a couple guys from China (who, unlike me, spoke Italian fluently). While I patiently waited, I lost myself exploring the stacks. There had to be thousands of old texts and each book had a story to tell beyond what was just written in its pages. I didn't even realize that several hours went by before my time eventually came.

Finally, it was my chance to not just experience the books with my untrained eye, but with the help of Marco, the guardian of the bookshop. While he couldn't really speak English, and I couldn't really speak Italian, we were able to somehow communicate. I just hoped I didn't accidentally agree to buy a $10,000 book. I spent even more time just browsing the oldest volumes, slowly becoming surer and surer hat my ultimate path was to buy a book.

After exploring the different subjects, feeling as much like a Renaissance sage as a high schooler can, I kept coming back to one book. A Latin translation of a work by the Greek rhetorician Hermogenes of Tarsus, printed in 1560 in Basel, Switzerland, and bound in simple parchment. And no, I don't speak or read Latin either. Aside from its beauty, it was one of the oldest books in the shop. Holding it was not just holding a piece of the Renaissance, but a piece of every moment it has lived through to this day.

BE ARTICULATE *AND* CONCISE. THAT'S A GREAT WAY TO PIQUE THE READER'S INTEREST. ALSO, THINK ABOUT THE SUBTEXT BEING CONVEYED TO COLLEGES: THE WRITER IS INSIGHTFUL AND HAS A STRONG SENSE OF CURIOSITY. THESE ARE TRAITS THAT COLLEGES LOVE TO SEE IN STUDENTS.

The more I looked at it, the more I loved it. The only thing that wasn't so attractive was the 300-euro price. Buying the book would be a vicious blow toward years of savings from odd jobs and birthdays. But it was too late—leaving the shop without it was unfathomable. Since the initial pain of making the largest purchase of my life, I've never regretted it.

One of my friends laughed and told me she couldn't justify buying a $30 book, let alone one for $300. Yet, seeing it on my desk every day in its protective clear case only reinforces the meaning it holds for me and the way it has lasted through the ages.

To say I came away with an amazing piece of history doesn't even tell the full story. I came away with a physical memory of the experience—standing on the unstable ladder against the shelves, conversing with a man with whom I didn't even share a language, and getting a picture with the guys from China just because I was a part of their experience too.

Yes, the book itself may "only" be 462 years old, but the memories it contains, from the 16th century up to my own, last forever.

Mira M.

New Jersey

Cornell University

> THE LESSONS WE TAKE FROM OBSTACLES WE ENCOUNTER CAN BE FUNDAMENTAL TO LATER SUCCESS. RECOUNT A TIME WHEN YOU FACED A CHALLENGE, SETBACK, OR FAILURE. HOW DID IT AFFECT YOU, AND WHAT DID YOU LEARN FROM THE EXPERIENCE?

IDEAS

Regarded as perhaps the most orthodox precursor of womanhood, my first period was a moment I had long awaited. You would think that the women plastered across Advil containers crouched over in agony would deter me from galvanizing such an event—but I could not have been more engrossed.

I relished the idea of no longer harboring the body of the stick-thin prepubescent girl susceptible to mockery—the punchline of judgemental middle-schooler's jokes in the gym locker rooms. If my body could just mimic that of a woman, I could grow up. Right?

Since the age of 7, that body resulted in a grooming for swimming stardom. In fact, I was one of the best swimmers in New Jersey: my first state title at age 10, my first national cut at age 13. Spending nearly 3 hours at the pool every day since my early teens, swimming became my young adult life: my passion; my purpose. I wanted to be great.

About a month after my first national competition, I finally experienced some physical change—finally able to replace my once ridiculed training bra with a supportive underwire. Finally a woman.

However, in the weeks following, my once anticipated relief was overshadowed by a sequence of unsatisfactory practices—ones where I began to experience overexhaustion and prototypical fatigue. That fatigue bled into other aspects of my life; it became hard to focus in school and to work with others. My self-confidence dwindled.

Weeks bled into years; eventually any mention of a "good" race or a "good" meet was referred to in the past tense. The very transition I thought would carry me into womanhood stripped me of my future. Why did becoming a woman have to be at the expense of my greatest passion?

I hated being a woman. Well, that was until I redefined what being woman truly is. I looked to my Mother, a woman who devoted over 10 years to higher-level learning and further educating women at the college level; I learned that being a strong woman is using the privileges of a rigorous education to support, inspire, and educate others.

I looked to my Aunt, a woman working in a predominantly male-dominated finance industry; I learned that being a strong woman is the ability to persist and encourage other women to combat societal norms and pressures.

I looked to my Great Aunt, a woman who worked as a nurse, not just in hospitals, but physically on the battlefields in the Vietnam War; I learned that being a strong woman is possessing unforgiving selflessness to heal others before myself.

And lastly, I looked to the mirror, reflecting on the little girl that fantasized about growing breasts, menstruating, and becoming an elite female athlete. For a long period of my life I felt that the process of physically morphing into a woman hindered my identity. Now, however, I wholeheartedly embrace my femininity which is a key component to my identity.

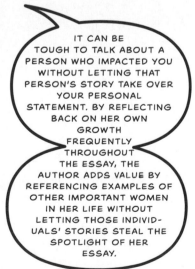

IT CAN BE TOUGH TO TALK ABOUT A PERSON WHO IMPACTED YOU WITHOUT LETTING THAT PERSON'S STORY TAKE OVER YOUR PERSONAL STATEMENT. BY REFLECTING BACK ON HER OWN GROWTH FREQUENTLY THROUGHOUT THE ESSAY, THE AUTHOR ADDS VALUE BY REFERENCING EXAMPLES OF OTHER IMPORTANT WOMEN IN HER LIFE WITHOUT LETTING THOSE INDIVID-UALS' STORIES STEAL THE SPOTLIGHT OF HER ESSAY.

I never quit swimming, in fact, I love to swim, but I do not define myself by my swimming accomplishments. I see that my self-worth is so much more than a medal around my neck or a trophy on my shelf; for, I exist to make positive change in the world around me.

Inspired by the woman before me, I vow to use a college-level education to teach, encourage, and support other women. I always wanted to grow up, and perhaps too quickly; but, I know now that my womanhood is not defined by the amount of weight on my chest or records on a scoreboard, but rather the positive impact I can make on other women.

Becoming a woman is not at all the journey I expected, but I am empowered just by checking "F" on my driver's license form. Fear me. I am a redefined woman. And I like me.

Naomi K.

Bethesda-Chevy Chase High School
Maryland

Northwestern University

SHARE AN ESSAY ON ANY TOPIC OF YOUR CHOICE.
IT CAN BE ONE YOU'VE ALREADY WRITTEN, ONE
THAT RESPONDS TO A DIFFERENT PROMPT,
OR ONE OF YOUR OWN DESIGN.

IDEAS

Glycerin, tiny pieces of fake snow, and glittering shards of glass scattered across the floor as the first snow globe fell. I swept up the pieces, tiny dots of blood on my hands as the glass nicked my fingers, and the snow globe sat turned on its side, a whole world turned into a sad chunk of stone in seconds.

I've been accumulating snow globes for as long as I can remember, carefully selecting the snow globe that best encapsulated my experiences when I was away from home. I kept the glass orbs on a small table in my room, and what began as only a few souvenirs soon became a crowded mess of memories.

I always thought snow globes were a great way to decorate my room, but it wasn't until I stumbled upon *The Loose Ends List* that I realized they were something more. When I read this book the summer before I started middle school, I learned a new term: "snow globe moments" – moments and memories that feel so surreal that they belong in a snow globe, freezing them in time to keep forever. While others describe their memories as mental snapshots, I view life as a series of snow globes: my favorite moments forever held within glass.

I store my physical snow globes in my room, which have now been relocated to their third spot, as my collection grew too big for my tiny table, and I accumulated too many books for my snow globes to afford real estate on my bookshelf. But I carry my snow globe moments with me, constantly turning them over and watching the snow sink down in my mind.

I began my collection with huge, elaborate snow globes, but I soon realized I could buy smaller ones and save room for more while still having something to commemorate an experience. Some of my snow globe moments are big, sparkling memories that fight to take up more space, but the small ones are no less important. Little things can be big, as some of the most mundane or uncomfortable moments are what I cherish most.

My great-grandmother's 100th birthday party righteously takes up an expanse of space on my mental shelf, as my younger self tried to conceptualize living for 100 years and how many snow globes my great-grandmother must have accumulated in that time. The memory of getting vomited on in an otherwise ordinary English class within my first month of high school, which was something seemingly small at the time – not to mention ridiculous and a bit horrifying – has had a more lasting impact by transitioning me into someone who isn't afraid to laugh at myself.

The good and the bad, the big and the small, the perfect and the messy, are all preserved in glass as my snow globes. I am the product of all my pasts, and instead of pushing away the snow globes that would be easier to avoid, I keep them on my shelf alongside my best moments. Everything I have ever done and everyone I have ever been teaches me to be the person I am today – someone who grows by remembering my mistakes and constantly seeks new adventures to put in snow globes.

After I cleaned up the mess the shattered snow globe had made, I picked up what remained: the inside, with nothing magical surrounding it, just the base and drab-looking interior. I contemplated tossing it along with the rest of what had once been, but I put it back on my shelf and still display it alongside the intact ones. My memories may shatter, fade, and dull, but the message I gained from them stays with me. No matter where I go or what I do, I have my snow globe moments.

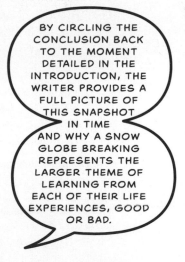

BY CIRCLING THE CONCLUSION BACK TO THE MOMENT DETAILED IN THE INTRODUCTION, THE WRITER PROVIDES A FULL PICTURE OF THIS SNAPSHOT IN TIME AND WHY A SNOW GLOBE BREAKING REPRESENTS THE LARGER THEME OF LEARNING FROM EACH OF THEIR LIFE EXPERIENCES, GOOD OR BAD.

Nidhi Sakpal
Mountain Lakes High School
New Jersey

Fordham University

Georgia Institute of Technology

Indiana University Bloomington

New Jersey Institute of Tech

Purdue University

Stevens Institute of Technology

The College of New Jersey

University of Wisconsin-Madison

Rutgers University

SOME STUDENTS HAVE A BACKGROUND, IDENTITY, INTEREST, OR TALENT THAT IS SO MEANINGFUL THEY BELIEVE THEIR APPLICATION WOULD BE INCOMPLETE WITHOUT IT. IF THIS SOUNDS LIKE YOU, THEN PLEASE SHARE YOUR STORY.

IDEAS

"Start packing, we're moving to New Jersey in two weeks"… Where is that state? The East Coast? West? Somewhere in the middle?

I come from a family that isn't afraid to pack up and relocate at a moment's notice. Since 2013, we've moved between nine homes and have had five relocations across three countries: India, the Netherlands, and the USA. Leaving friends and family behind never gets easier, no matter how many times I do it, and never having a permanent house or hometown has left me with an entirely different concept of 'home.'

BY GIVING THE READER HER FAMILY'S HISTORY OF MOVING, THE WRITER SETS THE SCENE FOR HER STORY. WE LEARN THAT HER DEFINITION OF "HOME" WILL BE UNIQUE.

Constantly relocating has allowed me to develop a multicultural identity and provided countless perspectives and experiences. If you glimpse into memories from my childhood, you'll find me setting up home after relocations, helping my mom to prepare food for Maharashtrian festivals, sometimes getting my hand burned by boiling oil. You'll come along on countless bike rides in Holland and pose with me beside every field of tulips we come across. However, being the 'new girl' was often difficult.

Colorism, racism, and sexism manifested themselves in the forms of bullying, backhanded compliments, and 'jokes.' Everything my Indian identity stood for was under judgment while living in predominantly white areas: the food I ate, the hairstyles and dresses I wore, and the festivals I celebrated, even the ones I didn't, became opportunities for slights and backhanded jokes. Furthermore, I recognized how marginalized young girls like myself were in school. Being one of three females and the only woman of color in my Data Structures class, a statistic others would mock, I despaired over the limited career opportunities I could hope for in the future.

Colorism and misogyny, which is overwhelmingly present in India, also manifest in my community: repeatedly asking my relatives to stop buying skin-bleaching creams and listening to condescending remarks my parents receive from friends and family about having two girls and not boys, are very real parts of my everyday life.

I try my best to be an advocate for change, which is important because I have a little sister who is now looking up to me during her freshman year and many other younger girls like her. Starting the Computer Science club to encourage girls to explore the CS field, joining the local Makerspace to help design products for inclusivity for the disabled community, and working for the Red Cross and other non-profits that align with my values, have all been an attempt to help others. I strive to be a part of the representation and support system for younger girls of color that I never had growing up. I've spent time in my counselor's and principal's offices reporting incidents of racism and homophobia and helped develop solutions to make our school safer for everyone– earning me the senior superlative 'Most Opinionated.' I also help keep my culture alive during school, wearing traditional lehengas during festivals, bringing kaju katlis and laddoos (Indian sweets) to school for my friends & teachers, and leading the Indian Cultural club to educate and celebrate all south Asian religions.

Over the years, I've had to heal from the bullying, and learning to live has become less about fitting in and more about being unapologetically myself. I'm not naive: I know my actions won't completely solve the issues threatening equality at my school or community. But my actions, no matter how small they may seem, serve to support those who face the same obstacles that I do. My multicultural identity is my badge that showcases my experiences, both the good and the unfair, that's helped shape my values, beliefs, and, ultimately, my childhood. I wouldn't be who I am had I not been pulled away from my many homes. I feel a little bit safer knowing I will always have a home, no matter where my future takes me, even if it takes me some time to create one.

Nitin Shah

La Costa Canyon High School
California

Harvard College

University of CA Berkeley

University of CA Los Angeles

Yale University

EVALUATE A SIGNIFICANT EXPERIENCE, ACHIEVEMENT, OR RISK THAT YOU HAVE TAKEN AND ITS IMPACT ON YOU.

IDEAS

CHRISTMAS IN INDIA

I never understood how my culture and background were different from everyone else's until a visit to my parents' mother country of India opened my eyes. Before that, I was just another kid in Southern California's suburban wilderness, in which parking spaces, large backyards, BMWs, and a strange sense of surrealism abound.

As I, age nine, stared out of the jumbo jet's window at the puffy white cloud tops and into the pale blue late December sky, I pondered back over the intense activities of the previous few days, including Christmas. That holiday was always perplexing for me as a child. Judging by what I could gather from my primary source of reliable information, cartoons, this Christmas thing involved a confused fat man forcing a bunch of moose to be his partners in crime as he broke into people's homes only to leave things, instead of take them. The most puzzling feature of all to me, as a San Diegan, was that white substance everyone was walking in and building real live snowmen out of.

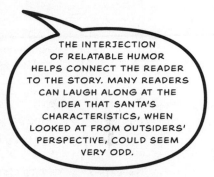

THE INTERJECTION OF RELATABLE HUMOR HELPS CONNECT THE READER TO THE STORY. MANY READERS CAN LAUGH ALONG AT THE IDEA THAT SANTA'S CHARACTERISTICS, WHEN LOOKED AT FROM OUTSIDERS' PERSPECTIVE, COULD SEEM VERY ODD.

It was all oddly interesting, but what did all this have to do with me? I asked my mother, my backup data source. Christmas, she told me, can mean certain things to certain people, but to most people, it's a religious day. Is that what it is for us? I asked. No, she said flatly. Upon further pressing, all she would say was that we believed different things than some people. She would not explain those different things, though. My parents never did much explaining; they preferred rather that my sister and I figure things out for ourselves in our own way.

Things in India were a far cry different from back home. This was apparent from the moment we departed from the airport into a hot Bombay night so muggy there was no need to stop for a drink; I need only open my mouth to take in all the moisture I would need.

It was like this, with my mouth and eyes and ears wide open, that I took in the tastes and sights and sounds of India, conscious for the first time of my background and identity. I watched from a filthy, rust-covered train as a tiny cross-section of Indian life passed me by, a virtual slide show of the people here and their way of life, much removed from my own.

Dozens of dark-skinned naked children, many about my age, engaged in a playful shoving match in a waist-high brown-colored river. They cared not about getting dirty or sick or about the passing train they undoubtedly saw many times a day; their only care was about the moment. On an overlooking hill, old and wrinkled women watched them coolly in the sweltering heat as they milked cows and swiftly unleashed words that I could not have understood even had I been able to hear them over the train's drone and the children's screaming. Nearby, the women's husbands repaired the proud yet cramped dried-mud homes that stood chipped and battered from a recent earthquake. The men functioned as a single unit, concentrating completely on one building before moving on to the next. The entire village had perhaps twenty of these constructs, and the cows and bulls grazing in the surrounding pasture seemed to outnumber the people 2-to-1.

I realized that this place, not the life back home, was where I really came from, yet I was still awed with the people's contentment. They had so little in the way of material possessions, yet were so happy. They didn't need a car, or fence, or swanky home to be satisfied. Every day was their Christmas, and the gift was life.

Olivia D.

New Jersey

Brown University

Pepperdine University

Reed College

University College Dublin

University of St. Andrews

DISCUSS AN ACCOMPLISHMENT, EVENT, OR REALIZATION THAT SPARKED A PERIOD OF PERSONAL GROWTH AND A NEW UNDERSTANDING OF YOURSELF OR OTHERS.

IDEAS

I made the decision to dye my hair. While I tried to assure my mom that the decision was far from impulsive, truthfully I was struggling to convince myself. I had felt stuck for so long: Stuck in my house, in a routine I hated, in a time where I did not have control. And so, in an effort to take control, that next morning I went to the salon and asked to add just a few burgundy highlights to my natural brown hair. Subtle, yet still fun and new. A few hundred dollars, the wrong shade of dye, and five hours later however, I walked out with bright pink hair. But, for the sake of cost and my dignity, I pretended to love it.

For a while, all I did was pretend. I pretended to feel okay even though I was just as stuck as before, only now my hair was pink. I had no choice, so I lived with it, or rather, lived despite it. As it turns out, however, bright pink is pretty difficult to ignore and tends to turn heads in public. Nevertheless, being the generally shy, closed off person I was, I strived to brush off any comments and continued to ignore it.

Just under a month after getting it dyed, a lovely old woman rushed up to me in a store and complimented my hair. In my typical fashion, I turned and thanked her with a quick smile when she audibly gasped. She proceeded to tell me how much she loved my teeth and how they were perfect. While I was certainly thankful that someone appreciated the grueling years I had spent with braces, I did not quite know how to reply. But to be polite I thanked her again, and began a conversation. In response to this small polite gesture, she gave me a moment of love and compassion. She told me about her granddaughters and of her life at my age, and she listened to me with care and interest. She gave me a moment of intimate connection, not out of obligation, but out of pure kindness. It was one of the strangest and most beautiful interactions I have ever had with another person.

I began to open myself up and not write off the comments I received. I allowed myself to have conversations like this one time and time again, all beginning with people who had simply approached to comment on my hair. For the first time, I felt seen and heard in a way I never had with my natural hair. And so, when the pink began to fade, I dyed it again in my bathroom sink. I was not ready to move on from pink hair just yet.

BY USING A METAPHOR TO CONNECT PINK HAIR TO PERSONAL GROWTH, THE AUTHOR WEAVES A DEEPER MESSAGE THROUGHOUT THEIR ESSAY TELLING STORIES, SUCH AS CONNECTING WITH A STRANGER AT THE STORE, THAT MANY READERS CAN RELATE TO.

People are hesitant to talk to one another, often too afraid of the risk of rejection and embarrassment that comes with putting themselves out there. They look for an excuse to interact with those around them. For the next eight months, I kept my hair pink to be that excuse. I broke out of the small world that I had been stuck in and connected with the people around me. I learned to love pink hair.

Eventually, dyeing my hair became too much, and I let the pink fade to a bleach blonde. I was sad at first, but I was ready to let go. I knew that even without it, I carry every lesson that having pink hair taught me. I try every day to go out of my way and interact with the people around me, even when they no longer have an excuse to talk to me. I understand what it feels like to not only be seen, but to see others. I hope with every stranger's story I listen to, someone gets to feel that same joy I feel: that someone, with no obligation to, sees you.

Philip James Madelen Rucker

St. Andrew's School
Georgia

Boston College

Brown University

Emory University

Tufts University

Tulane University

University of Rochester

Yale University

WE ASK YOU TO WRITE A PERSONAL ESSAY THAT WILL HELP US TO KNOW YOU BETTER. WRITE ABOUT WHAT MATTERS TO YOU, AND YOU ARE BOUND TO CONVEY A STRONG SENSE OF WHO YOU ARE.

IDEAS

MY MOMENT OF RECKONING

The blistering sun shines through the tall fir trees onto a mound of frosty snow that sparkles like diamonds. As the heat of the summer day melts the snow, the snow forms a stream that curls down the hillside onto the quiet road below. I walk up the hillside with my skates over my shoulder, the sun shining on my black pants. It is hot. I enter the rink to the familiar sounds of sharp blades etching the ice to the beat of Beethoven. Indoors, the air is chilly; the ice is glistening; the heat from outside meets the icy coolness of the rink at the tall, wide windows.

> THE USE OF DETAILED IMAGERY IN THE INTRODUCTION IMMEDIATELY HOOKS THE READER AND PAINTS A PICTURE OF THE ICE RINK AND SURROUNDING SNOWY HILLSIDE.

Hour after hour, day after day, the same Zamboni brings white snow from inside the rink to the outside, dumping it into the same spot, creating the same flowing stream down the hillside. Seen from outdoors, the mound of snow is an aberration in the summer heat, but seen through the windows from indoors the same snow, framed by the trees, suggests a crisp, sunny, winter day. Even though the snow has been there every morning since I started coming to this rink, it struck me on this particular morning both how lovely and how strange it appeared.

The snow is clean and fresh, the residue of the early morning practice of young, promising, and often famous, figure skaters. Not yet sullied like most snow by the time that it is taken away, it is still pristine. It clings to its frostiness in the hot sunshine – a futile effort. This snow has lived a short life. It began as the smooth, shimmering ice that first catches one's eye and then catches the edges of the skaters' blades. As the skaters worked harder,

> BY PERSONIFYING THE SNOW, THE WRITER IMPLIES THE IMPORTANCE THAT SNOW HAS HAD ON THEIR LIFE.

the ice became snow, and within an hour or two of its beginnings it was removed. The snow rests now in this mound like millions of tiny diamonds, vulnerable to the rays of the sun and awaiting its fate.

As I stop to notice the incongruous beauty of the snow, the evergreens, and the glaring summer sun, I reflect on an affinity that I feel towards this snow. I, like the snow, am a bit misplaced. It has been wonderful to be a part of the life at this beautiful rink, this elite training center that grooms champions, but it is not really my element. I long to be with my family and have a more "real" life, not the sheltered, specialized one that this rink offers, where one's purpose is so limited. I stare at the snow for a moment and consider that soon it will melt into water and flow down the hillside to regions uncertain. Yet, perhaps, it will land where water and snow naturally belong and where the season of its life fits the season of its setting. As I watch, I realize that, perhaps, it is time for me also to leave, to leave this rink and this rarefied life of competitive skating, to go down the hillside and return to my roots.

Rayna Hylden

D'Evelyn Junior/Senior High School
Colorado

Arizona State University

University of Colorado Boulder

University of Maryland

DISCUSS AN ACCOMPLISHMENT, EVENT, OR REALIZATION THAT SPARKED A PERIOD OF PERSONAL GROWTH AND A NEW UNDERSTANDING OF YOURSELF OR OTHERS.

IDEAS

After getting through 6.2 miles of the race, the last fifty yards couldn't be that hard—right? I had spent all summer training for the Tough Mudder 10k, and the last two hours of running through mud and nineteen obstacles was difficult, but I had done it. Yet when I saw that last obstacle, a thousand electric wires clicking at me, daring me to just turn around, I froze. In that moment I really had to ask myself, *how did I end up here*?

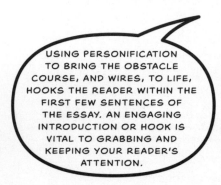

USING PERSONIFICATION TO BRING THE OBSTACLE COURSE, AND WIRES, TO LIFE, HOOKS THE READER WITHIN THE FIRST FEW SENTENCES OF THE ESSAY. AN ENGAGING INTRODUCTION OR HOOK IS VITAL TO GRABBING AND KEEPING YOUR READER'S ATTENTION.

Most of my growth in my life has been deciding to do hard things. Sometimes that means taking an intense course load, sometimes it's pushing out of my comfort zone to try out a new interest.

And sometimes it means running through live wires to finish the 10k obstacle course I had signed up for months earlier. Up until that point, I considered myself somebody who wasn't too affected by fear. I started rock climbing as a kid, so heights were never an issue. Performing and public speaking didn't bother me, as years of music and theater had trained me to surpass that. Even when I've had to deal with emergencies, I was able to take action in the moment and just get through it. Of course I had felt scared, but until faced with that last challenge of the race, I had never felt so completely frozen.

After some deep breaths and a pep talk from the obstacle attendant, I started my last sprint through the wires. It took a couple steps for me to actually get hit, but that first shock was no joke. My mind stopped, but my body just kept going. I got to the other side where my cousin waited for me, and we crossed the finish line together.

While enjoying the finish line festivities, I couldn't help but keep thinking about how difficult overcoming a new fear really is, and it was the first time in a very long time that I had been forced to face that. It made me remember why I loved to run that extra mile or throw out an attempt at a climb far above my skill level—those things give me the chance to prove to myself that yes, I *can*. I initially started running and lifting weights to deal with mental health issues, and eventually that mentality became second nature. When I can prove my physical strength, I find a lot more confidence in my mental strength. Though I can't say I enjoyed running through a series of live wires, it gave me a much-needed challenge and reminder that I can overcome anything I have the determination to do.

Having that moment of clarity became especially important as I entered my marching band season as head drum major. Our director resigned two weeks before the start of the season, and I needed to be strong for myself and my band. I've had to rely on that strength this season more than ever as I've led student leadership and the band as a whole through the difficulties of a director change, and remembering why I choose to do hard things helped me more than I could've imagined. Even when facing uncertainty or fear, I remember how much I have overcome in my past and carry that with me into my future. Life may be unpredictable and difficult at times, but fighting through that and having hope that something better lies on the other side has never failed me—I just need to get there and find out.

Sawyer Garrett

Valor College Prep
Tennessee

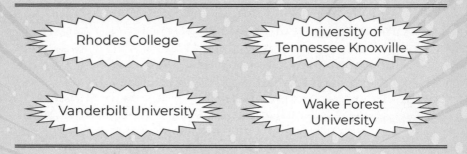

Rhodes College

University of Tennessee Knoxville

Vanderbilt University

Wake Forest University

THE LESSONS WE TAKE FROM OBSTACLES WE ENCOUNTER CAN BE FUNDAMENTAL TO LATER SUCCESS. RECOUNT A TIME WHEN YOU FACED A CHALLENGE, SETBACK, OR FAILURE. HOW DID IT AFFECT YOU, AND WHAT DID YOU LEARN FROM THE EXPERIENCE?

IDEAS

The environment in the locker room was as deadly as a gallon of brown recluse spider venom.

The seniors paraded around carrying their jugs, force feeding it to younger players. They delivered the toxin through comments like, "F*** you, b****," or through pushing freshmen out of the way, and it was lethal to the Valor Collegiate basketball team.

> THE WRITER'S USE OF A SIMILE ENHANCES THE STORY AND REVEALS HIS WRITING SKILLS.

Culture had been a problem since my freshman season, when we were losing nearly every game. There I was, dutifully warming the bench, and—like the mouse not stirring on Christmas Eve—I quietly observed the omnipresent problematic behaviors in the sophomore class. The next season was not much better. I was extremely reserved and just tried to maintain good standing with those older (and bigger) than me.

Then, my junior year came around and I decided that, as an upperclassman, it was my obligation to subtly set a good example for the new freshmen through quiet leadership. However, I was prepared to just sit and watch the seniors again because it was their last season with the team and anything they did this year, I thought, wouldn't impact the program in the long-run. (And, like I said, they were all bigger than me.)

Then senior night happened. The game started alright, with us leading 20-18. But by the start of the second period, things started to cascade downhill. The first domino was our defense not being able to stop the opponent. Next, one of the seniors wasn't where he was supposed to be; another player yelled at him, and they began to exchange F-bombs on court like they were at a Chamber of Commerce Mixer. Coach immediately pulled them. One took his jersey off and stormed off to the locker room. As coach realized there was no hope for this dumpster-fire of a game, remaining seniors were subbed out. As they came off, they slouched down, arms folded in their chair (if they hadn't already flipped it), pouting, and cussing at those still engaged in the game. All of them were suspended.

Sitting on the bench during that game, thinking to myself how frustrated I was with the culture, I knew that the seniors' actions in the present *would* have massive ramifications for years to come in the form of older players continuing to feel entitled and harassing the younger players. I needed to do something.

After the game, I thought back to a prior interaction I had with the Athletic Director at the Special Olympics about the basketball season. He had admired my efforts with the younger players, noting how I had consistently encouraged them and been a team player. Towards the end of the conversation, he said something resembling, "No wonder you are the captain." I felt so honored (even though there wasn't an official captain). Then, it hit me: I had the antidote for the toxin. I drafted a team "code of arms," detailing how team players should act and what behaviors are "toxic." Then, once I organized a time to share this with the team, I discussed my points and committed to call out issues when they first arise. The seniors, to my surprise, listened intently, committed to hold up their end, and poured out every last drop of their toxins. Ultimately, we had the most unified practices and games the program had ever had.

BY REFERENCING AN ANTIDOTE AND TOXIN, THE WRITER CONNECTS TO HIS OPENING LINE AND ADDS CONTINUITY TO THE STORY.

I realized courage and leadership can be most powerful when someone speaks out to support progress. I'm an aspiring teacher. I will use my newfound bravery and vocality not just in my senior season, but also in my future career. An educator's job is to equip students with skills – such as compassion, leadership, acceptance of diversity, inclusion, bravery, and so much more – necessary to counteract toxins in their own lives. I know what I've learned through basketball will allow me to succeed in that role.

Tom D.

Seton Hall Preparatory
New Jersey

Boston College

SHARE AN ESSAY ON ANY TOPIC OF YOUR CHOICE.
IT CAN BE ONE YOU'VE ALREADY WRITTEN, ONE
THAT RESPONDS TO A DIFFERENT PROMPT,
OR ONE OF YOUR OWN DESIGN.

IDEAS

"ROOM 6125"

I retreated to room 6125 after a seemingly endless day of anguish. As I paced through the monochromatic room that had become home for the past three months, I locked eyes with the one constant in my life: my journal. After an emotionally heavy day, I looked forward to reflecting on my experiences. Opening my journal, as teardrops of fear and resentment leaped off my face, I wrote, *I never want to practice medicine.*

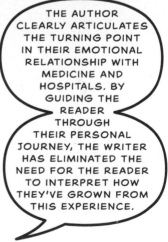

A hospital can be a dark place. The groans of the immunocompromised bounce off the concrete walls, and the depressing, sterile atmosphere can appear dreadful. Every day, my traditionally joyful 45-year-old father was sent through rounds of chemotherapy for Multiple Myeloma. Gradually, his hair vanished strand by strand, falling onto the floor with the grace of a snowflake. His skin turned pale, contrasting his previously dark Mediterranean skin. Before my eyes, I saw my hero fall from grace, and it pained me to see the shell of the man I looked up to. Cancer was his kryptonite. This constant cycle of bloodwork, labs, chemotherapy, and doctor's visits rendered me both frustrated and angry.

As a means of therapy in a seemingly hopeless situation, I escaped to my journal. It was a safe space amidst a battlefield of emotion and conflict. I began to take particular notes on what I had seen during the day: the different people I encountered, the atmosphere of the hospital, the results of labs, and essentially every working part of the hospital. I started to realize my experiences were the catalyst in my progression from a worried, anxious person to one who built confidence that remission was within reach.

THE AUTHOR CLEARLY ARTICULATES THE TURNING POINT IN THEIR EMOTIONAL RELATIONSHIP WITH MEDICINE AND HOSPITALS. BY GUIDING THE READER THROUGH THEIR PERSONAL JOURNEY, THE WRITER HAS ELIMINATED THE NEED FOR THE READER TO INTERPRET HOW THEY'VE GROWN FROM THIS EXPERIENCE.

Hearing the daily conversations between doctors, nurses, and hospital staff engaged and motivated me to learn more about medicine.

As Spring transitioned into Summer, I buried myself in medical textbooks and journals, learning about human anatomy and the nomenclature of medical diagnoses and procedures. Every opportunity I had, I surrounded myself with doctors and nurses, longing to gain insight on their careers. I would scour the internet for hours, sometimes falling asleep to the enthralling TED Talks and lectures hosted by many of the brightest minds in our society. After gathering information from different sources in the medical field, my process would then be to synthesize anecdotes into several of my journals. The narratives gave me a newfound sense of comfort; partly because I could better comprehend my father's diagnosis and prognosis, but also, because my heart told me I was making a difference in my father's life.

I discovered optimism in my father's situation by furthering my interest in the medical field and finding a passion for orthopedics. Predominantly fueled by repeated knee and ankle injuries, my interest in orthopedics also came from a fascination with the musculoskeletal system and participation in the Future Medical Leaders Club at school. I have shadowed several orthopedic surgeons, learned about different terminology and diagnoses, witnessed procedures, and volunteered for nonprofits, aiding those with foot and ankle ailments in underdeveloped areas over three weeks. After medical school, I aspire to impact the lives of those in need and change the longstanding stigma of the medical field from a place of fear to hope, along with promoting the importance of good mental health within medicine.

My father is in remission four years later, and I occasionally accompany him to the hospital. Recently, while walking through the hospital's hallways, I stumbled across a familiar place: room 6125. Stepping into the empty room, I felt the same desire for reflection and confession I had four years prior. I opened my backpack and pulled out the one constant in my life. As tears of joy and satisfaction fell off my face, I opened my journal and began to write.

Xueyang (Sean) Li
Northview High School
Georgia

Cornell University

Dartmouth College

Duke University

Emory University

Georgia Institute of Technology

Northwestern University

Princeton University

University of Georgia

Washington University in St. Louis

WRITE ON A TOPIC OF YOUR CHOICE.

IDEAS

Every day, the news is filled with stories of brilliant politicians and gorgeous Hollywood actors. Society chooses to give its million-dollar bills to football players and pop stars, and even my parents want me to jump on the bandwagon of fame and wealth by becoming a lawyer, a neurosurgeon, or a business magnate. Yet somehow, I know I would not feel quite right spending my life as a glamorous celebrity or an affluent doctor, but I hope to be a somebody someday. After all, who doesn't want to make their mom and dad proud?

Throughout my life, I have always asked myself the question that all adults ask kids, "What do you want to be when you grow up?" Back when I was five, I was thrilled with the thought of being a farmer, growing my own food in my own backyard. That quickly changed, however, especially after I realized how cool it would be to own a gas station and whiff that gasoline odor all day. But even something as awesome as that could not interest me forever, and I quickly went through other stages when I decided to become an astronomer, a lawyer, and a marine biologist.

But until now, I never even considered aspiring to be like those who I have had most contact with throughout my life — teachers. Looking back, I can still smell the six-molar ammonia when Dr. Warren stayed after school for two extra hours just so we could finish up our AP Chemistry labs. I can still taste the donuts that Mr. Tomlin bought those Saturday mornings when he drove us to middle school Academic Bowl tournaments. And I can still recall those warm afternoons when my kindergarten teacher, Mrs. Osteen, randomly stopped by my house just to say "hi." Such are the teachers who have shaped my character these past twelve years

BY USING SHORT ANECDOTES, THE WRITER CONVEYS THE REASONS THAT HAVE LED THEM TO CHOOSING TEACHING AS THEIR FUTURE CAREER PATH. THIS "SHOW, DON'T TELL" STYLE OF WRITING IS MORE ENGAGING AND INSIGHTFUL FOR THE READER.

in school, and such are the teachers who build the foundations of our communities, guiding the paths of those who become our divas and CEOs. Such are the teachers who are my heroes.

Little boys and girls always say they want to be like their heroes some day, and as a boy still growing up, I hope to be like my heroes one day - not a wealthy NBA player or a distinguished Congressmen, but just an ordinary teacher. I have actually thought about it for quite some time. As a tutor of my school and a past teaching assistant at Kumon Math and Reading Center, I have had my share of teaching, and I know how rewarding it is. Still vivid in my mind is the voice of pure joy when one of my students called to thank me for helping her get a four on the AP Chemistry exam. In the background, I could hear her mom screaming to offer me homemade chocolate chip cookies. Furthermore, I dream of being a teacher because I know how delightful it feels to see those light bulbs pop on. I still remember aiding an algebra student in grasping logarithm concepts one day. Everyone had left school already, and it was just my tutee and I in the classroom. Both of us were dead tired, but I knew I would go home unsatisfied without my tutee understanding the change of base rule. After I explained the concept for the ninth time, he suddenly jumped up and shouted "got'em!" and I knew I would drive back home content that evening.

And finally, those grateful "thank-you's" and expensive coffee baskets on the last day of the semester – I have had my experiences of those, and I know how gratifying it feels, like you are on top of the world because you have made a difference in someone's life, that you are not only a teacher but a somebody after all.

Anonymous 1
New Jersey

Duke University

DISCUSS AN ACCOMPLISHMENT, EVENT, OR REALIZATION THAT SPARKED A PERIOD OF PERSONAL GROWTH AND A NEW UNDERSTANDING OF YOURSELF OR OTHERS.

IDEAS

UNPLUGGED

It was the morning of my sixth birthday. I took to the stage with my band behind me and stared out into the crowd of over 1,000 fans. Their deafening cheers made it hard to hear our drummer counting down. I was opening the show with the guitar solo from "Sweet Child O' Mine" by Guns N' Roses' legendary guitarist, Slash. As my fingers danced on the guitar, my virtual audience roared, marking the beginning of my Guitar Hero III passion. I devoted hours to memorizing Slash's renowned guitar licks, and my love for Rock n' Roll was born. I wondered what it would be like to be a real rock star performing on a *real* stage.

THIS HOOK GRABS THE READER'S ATTENTION AND INSPIRES THEM TO CONTINUE READING THE ESSAY. A STRONG HOOK IS A CRITICAL COMPONENT OF EVERY SUCCESSFUL PERSONAL STATEMENT.

Ten years later, on my sixteenth birthday, I upgraded to my first *real* guitar and amp. Every night, I would make time to balance my schoolwork with the excitement of mimicking Slash's fingers sliding up and down the fretboard. My guitar was my escape from the daily pressures of high school. For a long time, I kept my hobby a secret. It felt natural to jam for my Guitar Hero virtual fans who cheered for me unconditionally, but I was terrified at the thought of playing in front of a live audience. In fact, when I bought my amp, I made sure it came with a headphone port so that I could plug in my headphones and practice silently without the fear of being judged. While plugged in, my insecurities were inaudible.

Early in my junior year, while on a school trip, I visited the Rock & Roll Hall of Fame. Friends who knew about my secret passion taunted me to pick up the guitar that was on display and "show them" something. Never having played in front of anyone, let alone my friends, I became overwhelmed with anxiety. Nevertheless, I indulged them. I fumbled as I began to play. The dissonance of the notes was harsh and my friends cackled, "That sounds pretty bad. I thought he said he taught himself how to play the guitar. He's been practicing for months?" Their disparaging comments replayed in my head all night. I felt embarrassed and hurt. Maybe my friends were right? Despite my humiliation, I continued to practice, ensuring my headphones were securely plugged into my amp.

A few weeks later, while jamming in my room one night, I received a text from my dad complimenting me on my guitar playing. Confused, I looked down at my amp. I forgot to plug in my headphones. Mortified, I reached for the cord but then hesitated. I realized how apprehensive and insecure I had become and didn't want to continue hiding my music. I no longer wanted the opinions of others to make me feel stressed and uneasy. If I was ever going to perform on a real stage, I had to break free of my inhibitions and practice out loud.

By the end of junior year, I had become very motivated to take my guitar playing to the next level. I decided to perform Guns N' Roses' "Sweet Child O' Mine" in our high school's Battle of the Bands. I assembled a band and we practiced. Within one month, we were ready for battle. As I took to the stage, I shielded my eyes from the spotlights that illuminated me. I anxiously surveyed the crowd. Over 1,000 students and teachers were awaiting our performance. Suddenly, my guitar felt heavy and clumsy in my cramped hands. I panicked. I imagined for a moment that I was Slash, my guitar hero, and inhaled deeply. I smiled and relaxed as I exhaled. Our drummer ticked down and my fingers began to dance along the fretboard. The crowd roared. My virtual fantasy had become reality. I felt secure and proud. For the very first time, *I was unplugged.*

THE WRITER CONCLUDES HIS ESSAY BY CIRCLING BACK TO HIS INTRODUCTION. THIS WRITING TECHNIQUE ADDS CONTINUITY TO THE STORY.

Anonymous 2

New Jersey

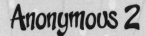

University of Denver

THE LESSONS WE TAKE FROM OBSTACLES WE ENCOUNTER CAN BE FUNDAMENTAL TO LATER SUCCESS. RECOUNT A TIME WHEN YOU FACED A CHALLENGE, SETBACK, OR FAILURE. HOW DID IT AFFECT YOU, AND WHAT DID YOU LEARN FROM THE EXPERIENCE?

IDEAS

"The Best Exercise"

I have always been told by my friends and family that I have a gift when it comes to self-discipline, self-control, and determination. After fracturing my back freshman year of high school, I replaced competitive sports with fitness, in particular, weight training. After my back injury, the following months were the most emotionally, academically, physically, and spiritually challenging of my life. I was diagnosed with mild anxiety and depression. I turned to fitness and weight training as an outlet to clear my mind and release the stress that accumulated inside me. My determination to get better and intense focus on fitness strengthened my mental and physical energies and gave me the confidence to attack my anxiety and depression head-on. It has since become the most essential part of my life. I taught myself the science of nutrition and formed new habits to complement my weight training. Within one year, I felt better than I ever had both mentally and physically. Until then, I never truly realized the power of self-control, self-discipline, and determination.

WHILE WRITING ABOUT ANXIETY AND DEPRESSION CAN BE RISKY, THE WRITER DIMINISHES THE RISK BY QUICKLY TELLING US THAT HE BATTLED THIS CHALLENGE AND WON THROUGH WEIGHT TRAINING.

My family was proud of my progress and continued to encourage me. My dad at the time had growing health concerns and desperately needed to lose weight. Inspired by my own transformation, he came to me for help. I realized this was a calling not only to coach him but also to connect with him through my love for fitness. I emphasized the importance of developing and maintaining a dedicated workout routine and a sustainable nutrition plan. I explained that simply going to the gym wouldn't yield results. He had to be consistent, push limits, and strive to make each week greater than the last. I stressed to him the importance of healthy eating and making good food choices. My dad embraced my help and committed to reclaiming his health. We trained daily, took trips to the grocery store, studied nutrition and ingredients, and planned balanced meals. Within one year, he shed 60 pounds.

My dad often reminds me of how rewarding the process has been for him, but truthfully it has been just as rewarding for me. Witnessing someone I love and admire take such initiative has been extremely inspiring. I realize that self-discipline is a skill. I appreciate how empowering this has felt not only for me but for my entire family. Coaching my family and friends to make good choices and adopt healthier lifestyles has also been so gratifying. They feel better about themselves, overcome life's obstacles, and better manage stress and anxiety.

My intense passion for fitness together with my self-discipline has fueled me to be the greatest version of myself both mentally and physically and has proven to be the single best exercise against anxiety and depression.

You've seen a wide range of prompts in this book; as you start your own application, you'll need to figure out which ones are available to you, and of those, which is best suited for the essay that you want to write. Here are some additional types of prompts you may see, specifically from individual schools.

The "Why College X" Essay

You'll see this prompt phrased in several different ways:

- What about being a student at College X most excites you?

- What do you value most about College X?

- What motivated you to apply to College X?

- Beyond rankings, location, and athletics, why are you interested in College X?

This last example is very telling. Let us assure you that no college wants to hear about any of those things in your response.

It's your job to identify specific programs and activities, coursework, professors, opportunities, and aspects of the school's academic and social landscape that excite you. Don't make the mistake of rushing through your research or replicating the content for different schools. Your response should convince the school that you're the perfect fit for them and they're the perfect fit for you. Take your time to dig into the school's website and other valuable resources. Imagine you're a student at that college and clearly illustrate what your presence will be like on campus.

The "Academic Interest" Essay

You'll see this prompt phrased in several different ways:

- Describe how you plan to pursue your academic interest at College X.

- Describe your current intellectual interests and what makes them exciting.

- How will College X be the right environment to pursue your interests?

- Discuss your motivation for studying your selected major at our college.

This is your moment to clearly explain the evolution of your intellectual interests and how that specific college's academic programming will develop your mind and satisfy your intellectual curiosity.

If you have a good idea of your major and primary academic interest, dig deep into each school's website and identify professors, classes, concentrations, research institutes, clubs, and specific programming only offered at that particular institution. At the same time, if you are truly undecided—and it's OK if you are—be sincere about it. Since colleges know that most students will change their mind about their major at least once, be genuine and share your desire to explore majors while in college.

Don't simply repeat what you write about one school for another. Identify the unique aspects of that college that connect your specific intellectual interests and become an expert on how that school will meet your needs.

The "Community" Essay

You'll see this prompt phrased in different ways.

- We all exist within communities or groups of various sizes, origins, and purposes; pick one and tell us why it's important to you and how it shaped you.

- What was the environment in which you were raised?

- Describe your family, home, neighborhood, or community and explain how it has shaped you.

To answer the prompt, ask yourself, "Where is it that I feel the greatest sense of belonging?"

It may be an educational community like your IB cohort at your high school; a geographic community such as the community that exists when you grow up in a small town; or religious, ethnic, cultural, socioeconomic, or related to a specific hobby or interest.

Colleges are interested in what makes you feel connected to other people, and they want to get a sense of what shapes your beliefs and values, your hopes, and dreams. If you're going to be a contributing member of intellectual and social vitality on the campus, a college needs to predict what you might be involved in on campus and how you will positively impact the campus environment. What lasting contribution might you make? What role will you play and how will you fit in?

The "Meaningful Activity" Essay

You will see this prompt phrased a few different ways, such as:

- Briefly discuss the school or summer activity in which you have been the most involved.

- Briefly elaborate on one of your extracurricular activities.

You'll want to select an activity that explains one of your personal attributes that may not be illustrated in other areas of your application. If your main essay is focusing on resiliency, select an activity that shows a different positive quality that may not be exhibited in other parts of your application. Consider an activity that illustrates your commitment and your growth over time.

Avoid repeating details from your résumé or activity list. The point here is to identify what aspects of one activity have been meaningful to you. So, dig deep, and consider what you've learned about yourself, how you've grown, and what risks you've taken as an individual participating in this activity. College admissions officers love a good story, so even though these responses are typically short, try writing in a narrative format that captures and maintains the reader's attention.

Now that you've seen what other students in your shoes have done, and you've started to consider the types of prompts you can write for, the only thing left to do is to start writing. This doesn't mean that you have to generate a perfect, admission-worthy essay right this minute, the sort that we'd be proud to publish in future editions of this title. Remember, you're seeing the final versions of what these students worked hard to edit. But you *do* need to start generating ideas and trying out some of the techniques that you admire so that you can find a story and an approach that work for you. The following pages contain some activities and advice excerpted from our *Complete Guide to College Essays* book, which may help to further jumpstart your creative journey. For additional support with your essay or the entire application process, you can also explore the options available from some of the experts who helped select and annotate the essays for this volume at www.princetonreview.com/college-admissions/college-counseling.

IDENTIFYING YOUR AUDIENCE

Beware of commonly used topics.

Admissions staff are bored by essays which show little effort or provide little insight into an applicant. Submitting a grammatically sound essay is a start but is insufficient. The applicant's task is to reveal something new about him or her that he could not be easily discerned from a list of curricular and co-curricular activities.

—Earlham University

Despite the massive number of applications most colleges receive every year, certain essay topics come up frequently. In the recent past, for example, essays on service trips, athletic injuries, and the death of a loved one (grandparent, parent) topped the list.

We've said this before, but it can't hurt to repeat it: Admissions staff work diligently to approach each essay with the care and thought it deserves. *But they are only human.* If yours is the third essay they read *in one day* on how coming back from an injury motivated you to pull through tough times, they may mentally sigh and be unable to muster enthusiasm.

That's why it's always best to find topics that are unique to you—stories that other applicants couldn't tell, or at least couldn't phrase the same way—and which would therefore help you to be memorable.

To be clear, this doesn't mean that you can't still write about breaking your leg in a soccer game. It just means that you'll need to work even harder to elevate this essay above the others that may be just like it. If specific, stand-out details about your chosen prompt don't come readily to mind, you may want to choose a less-trodden path to go down.

FINDING YOUR PERFECT TOPIC

Sample Prompts from the 2023–2024 Common Application

1 Some students have a background, identity, interest, or talent so meaningful they believe their application would be incomplete without it. If this sounds like you, please share your story.

2 The lessons we take from obstacles we encounter can be fundamental to later success. Recount a time when you faced a challenge, setback, or failure. How did it affect you and what did you learn from the experience?

3 Reflect on a time when you questioned or challenged a belief or idea. What prompted your thinking? What was the outcome?

4 Reflect on something that someone has done for you that has made you happy or thankful in a surprising way. How has this gratitude affected or motivated you?

5 Discuss an accomplishment, event, or realization that sparked a period of personal growth and a new understanding of yourself or others.

6 Describe a topic, idea, or concept you find so engaging it makes you lose all track of time. Why does it captivate you? What or who do you turn to when you want to learn more?

7 Share an essay on any topic of your choice. It can be one you've already written, one that responds to a different prompt, or one of your own design.

BREAKING DOWN A PROMPT

For the most part, each prompt includes two to four questions, each of which must be fully answered. To make sure you stay on topic, break the prompt down into its separate components and respond to each question. Literally.

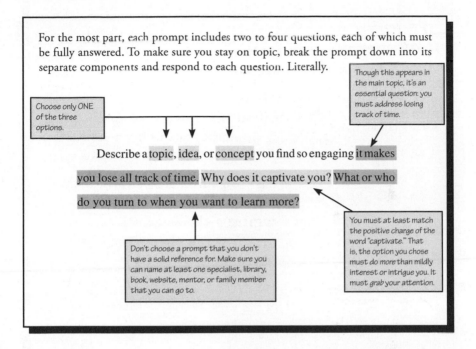

Though this appears in the main topic, it's an essential question: you must address losing track of time.

Choose only ONE of the three options.

Describe a topic, idea, or concept you find so engaging it makes you lose all track of time. Why does it captivate you? What or who do you turn to when you want to learn more?

Don't choose a prompt that you don't have a solid reference for. Make sure you can name at least one specialist, library, book, website, mentor, or family member that you can go to.

You must at least match the positive charge of the word "captivate." That is, the option you chose must do more than mildly interest or intrigue you. It must grab your attention.

ACTIVITY

Brainstorm the Pieces

Once you've broken down the prompt, start brainstorming options for your topic. Don't overthink it; just write a list of whatever comes to your mind. This is a pre-write to provide ideas for you to choose from. Below, we've demonstrated the sort of brainstorming we did on a specific topic for each prompt. Follow along and give yourself a few minutes to do your own brainstorming (on your own topic).

> Describe a topic, idea, or concept you find so engaging it makes you lose all track of time. Why does it captivate you? What or who do you turn to when you want to learn more?

Our brainstorming:

- physics
- eating
- dwarf stars
- cooking
- genealogy
- sleeping
- reading
- watching YouTube
- watching TED talks
- crafting
- gaming
- coding

Your brainstorming:

_____

_____

_____

_____

_____

_____

_____

_____

_____

_____

_____

_____

Though you'll only ultimately choose to write about one topic, idea, or concept, when you're brainstorming, don't set limits. You may have a concept in mind, but when you review the list you've written, you may realize that there's a more compelling idea.

DEVELOPING YOUR ESSAY

Fending off Writer's Block

Take a moment to think of your favorite three writers. Guess what? All three have probably experienced writer's block before! If you find yourself suffering from it, just remember that you're in good company, and that it doesn't at all reflect badly on you. What matters is what you do *next* to get past this block.

❶ Break your routine.

If you're stuck in a writing rut, break it. Get up from your chair. Grab a snack, go for a walk, take your mind away from the work. Don't treat this as an escape, though. It's not an excuse to start binging television or to avoid the work. Set a timer so you know when to get back to writing.

❷ Leave yourself hanging.

Think about how cliffhangers work on television or in books. They have you actively anticipating the next episode or chapter, ready to dive back in for more. You can also do this with your writing. Instead of exhausting every idea at once, end a session on an unfinished thought that you're excited to write about. Then, when you pick things back up, you'll already be ready to go.

❸ Jump around.

This isn't geometry. The shortest distance between two points doesn't have to be a straight line. If you're getting stuck on your introduction, jump to one of your paragraphs. If the conclusion is giving you grief, work on a different section.

❹ Talk it through.

If you can't bring yourself to pick up a pen, try recording yourself. Call up a friend or talk to a parent about what you're trying to do. Sometimes this can be enough to shake loose what you are trying to convey, or it might give you an idea for a new approach.

CHOOSING YOUR TONE

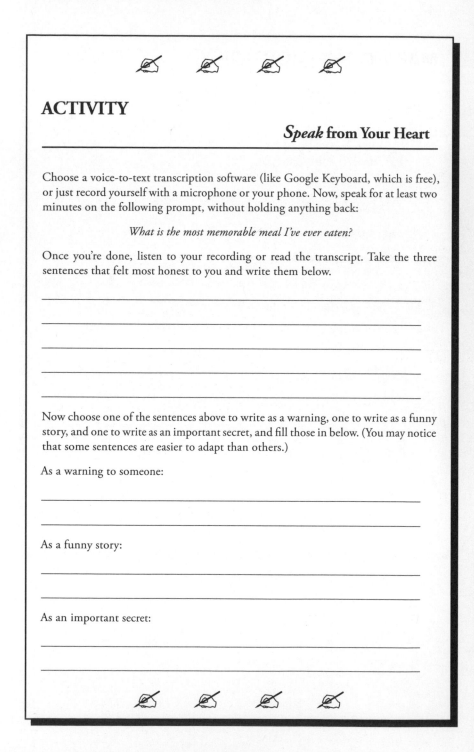

ACTIVITY

Speak from Your Heart

Choose a voice-to-text transcription software (like Google Keyboard, which is free), or just record yourself with a microphone or your phone. Now, speak for at least two minutes on the following prompt, without holding anything back:

What is the most memorable meal I've ever eaten?

Once you're done, listen to your recording or read the transcript. Take the three sentences that felt most honest to you and write them below.

_____

_____

_____

_____

_____

Now choose one of the sentences above to write as a warning, one to write as a funny story, and one to write as an important secret, and fill those in below. (You may notice that some sentences are easier to adapt than others.)

As a warning to someone:

_____

_____

As a funny story:

_____

_____

As an important secret:

_____

_____

KNOWING YOUR DRAFTS

MAKING THE MOST OF YOUR EDITORS

Once you have your editors, you'll need to send them your essay so that they can mark it up and give you feedback. But you may also want to prompt them to look for specific things, especially if they have differing areas of expertise, so that you can get the most out of them. After all, you don't just want them to run the same sort of spell-check that your word processing software can do!

Ask Them About More than Just the Grammar

You don't want to overwhelm your editors—they're doing you a favor, after all. But believe it or not, you'll actually be helping them if you provide them with a list of questions to think about *as* they read the essay. By all means, encourage your editors to give you separate feedback if they have any, but these targeted lists of questions will help them help you, and that's what any good editor wants to do.

- What is the main idea of the essay?

- Did it answer the question?

- Based on this essay, what do you know about me?

- What did this essay do well?

- Did the introduction catch your attention?

- How was the conclusion?

These questions will help you tackle the big picture and make sure that you essay is not just well written but also successful.

GRAMMAR AND WRITING TIPS

Grammar Chart

Grammatical Category	What's the Rule?	Bad Grammar	Good Grammar
Misplaced Modifier	A modifier is a word or phrase that describes something and should go right next to the thing it modifies.	1. Eaten in Mediterranean countries for centuries, **northern Europeans** viewed the tomato with suspicion. 2. A **former greenskeeper** now about to become the Masters champion, **tears** welled up in my eyes as I hit my last miraculous shot.	1. Eaten in Mediterranean countries, the tomato was viewed with suspicion by Northern Europeans. 2. I was a **former greenskeeper** who was now about to become the Masters champion; **tears** welled up in my eyes as I hit my last miraculous shot.
Pronoun Agreement	A pronoun must refer unambiguously to a noun, and it must agree in number with that noun.	1. Although **brokers** are not permitted to know executive access **codes, they** are widely known. 2. Unfortunately, both **candidates** for whom I worked sabotaged their own **campaigns** by accepting a **contribution** from illegal **sources.**	1. Although **brokers** are not permitted to know executive access **codes, the passwords** are widely known. 2. Unfortunately, both **candidates** for whom I worked sabotaged their own **campaigns** by accepting **contributions** from illegal **sources.**
Subject-Verb Agreement	The subject must always agree in number with the verb. Make sure you don't forget what the subject of a sentence is, and don't use the object of a preposition as a subject.	1. **Each** of the people involved in the extensive renovations **were** engineers. 2. Federally imposed **restrictions** on the ability to use certain information **has** made life difficult for lawbreakers.	1. **Each** of the people involved in the extensive renovations **was** an engineer. 2. Federally imposed **restrictions** on the ability to use certain information **have** made life difficult for lawbreakers.
Verb Tense	Always make sure your sentences' tenses match the time frame being discussed.	1. After he finishes working on his law school essays he **would go** to the party.	1. After he finishes working on his law school essays he **will go** to the party.

Grammar Chart—Continued

Grammatical Category	What's the Rule?	Bad Grammar	Good Grammar
Parallel Construction	Two or more ideas in a single sentence that are parallel need to be similar in grammatical form.	1. The two main goals of the Eisenhower presidency were a **reduction** of taxes and **to increase** military strength. 2. **To provide a child** with the skills necessary for survival in modern life is **like guaranteeing their** success.	1. The two main goals of the Eisenhower presidency were **to reduce** taxes and **to increase** military strength. 2. **Providing children** with the skills necessary for survival in modern life is **like guaranteeing their** success.
Comparisons	You can only compare things that are alike in category.	1. The **rules** of written English are **more stringent** than spoken **English.** 2. The **considerations** that led many colleges to impose admissions quotas in the last few decades **are similar to the quotas** imposed in the recent past by large businesses.	1. The rules of written English are **more stringent than those of** spoken English. 2. The **considerations** that led many colleges to impose admissions quotas in the last few decades **are similar to those** that led large businesses to impose quotas in the recent past.
Diction	There are many words that sound the same but mean different things.	1. Studying had a very positive **affect** on my score. 2. My high SAT score has positively **effected** the outcome of my college applications.	1. Studying had a very positive **effect** on my score. 2. My high SAT score has positively **affected** the outcome of my college applications.

Style Chart

Style Category	What's the Rule?	Bad Style	Good Style
Wordiness	Sentences should not contain any unnecessary words.	1. The medical school is accepting applications **at this point in time.** 2. She carries a book bag that is made out of leather **and textured.**	1. The medical school is accepting applications **now.** 2. She carries a **textured-leather** book bag.
Fragments	Sentences should contain a subject and a verb and express a complete idea.	1. I went to class. I went to the library.	1. I went to class and then I went to the library.
Run-ons	Sentences that consist of two independent clauses should be joined by the proper conjunction.	1. The test has a lot of difficult information **in it, you should** start studying right away.	1. The test has a lot of difficult information **in it, so you should** start studying right away.
Passive/Active Voice	Choose the active voice, in which the subject performs the action.	1. **The ball was hit by the bat.** 2. **My time and money were wasted** trying to keep www.justdillpickles.com afloat single-handedly.	1. **The bat hit the ball.** 2. **I wasted time and money** trying to keep www.justdillpickles.com afloat single-handedly.
Nonsexist Language	Sentences should not contain any gender bias.	1. A professor should correct **his** students' papers according to the preset guidelines. 2. From the beginning of time, **mankind** has used language in one way or another. 3. Are there any **upperclassmen** who would like to help students in their lit classes?	1. Professors should correct **their** students' papers according to the preset guidelines. 2. From the beginning of time, **humans** have used language in one way or another. 3. Are there any **seniors** who would like to help students in their lit classes?

INDEX

Though we recommend reading through all of the essays in this book—you never know what will inspire you—we have done our best to group them below by their closest Common Application prompt. Do not draw any conclusions about which prompt is "best" to answer based on the number of successful students in each group. If you have options on your application, choose the prompt that best allows you to express yourself.

PROMPTS:

Some students have a background, identity, interest, or talent so meaningful they believe their application would be incomplete without it. If this sounds like you, please share your story.

The lessons we take from obstacles we encounter can be fundamental to later success. Recount a time when you faced a challenge, setback, or failure. How did it affect you and what did you learn from the experience?

Reflect on a time when you questioned or challenged a belief or idea. What prompted your thinking? What was the outcome?

Reflect on something that someone has done for you that has made you happy or thankful in a surprising way. How has this gratitude affected or motivated you?

None of the essays we selected in this book matched this prompt.

Discuss an accomplishment, event, or realization that sparked a period of personal growth and a new understanding of yourself or others.

Describe a topic, idea, or concept you find so engaging it makes you lose all track of time. Why does it captivate you? What or who do you turn to when you want to learn more?

Share an essay on any topic of your choice. It can be one you've already written, one that responds to a different prompt, or one of your own design.

The two prompts below were written specifically for an individual college's application.